A Practical Guide to Fundraising and Public Relations

A Practical Guide to Fundraising and Public Relations

Veronica Canning

ICSA Publishing
The Official Publishing Company of
The Institute of Chartered Secretaries and Administrators

Published by ICSA Publishing Ltd
16 Park Crescent
London W1N 4AH

Typeset in 10/12pt Palatino
by Fakenham Photosetting Limited, Fakenham, Norfolk

Printed and bound in Great Britain
by MPG Books Ltd, Bodmin, Cornwall

British Library Cataloguing in Publication Data

A catalogue record for this book is available from
the British Library

ISBN 1–860720–51–X

This book is dedicated to my dear departed friend, Glenda Wilson, who was such a source of inspiration.

CONTENTS

ACKNOWLEDGEMENT

I would like to thank my husband, Peter, and children, Amber and Christopher, for their incredible help and support for the fundraiser in their life.

PREFACE

Why you should read this book

If you're reading this, then you are probably involved in fundraising, or planning to be. If so, this book is for you.

Imagine you have just completed a major fundraising event. You have exceeded your target, the chairperson of the fundraising committee actively led the project, the committee worked consistently hard, everyone pulled together, there were no hitches and you still went home everyday at 5 o'clock.

Now wake up. If only fundraising were that easy.

If you are involved in fundraising in any way you will know the reality is very different. Fundraising is a difficult and exhausting profession. I use the word 'profession' deliberately as there are so many dedicated, professional people working in the background with a fantastic range of skills all focused on the field of fundraising. Yet as a profession, fundraising is still in its infancy. This book is written primarily for people who work full-time in fundraising, whether they are the head of a fundraising department or a staff member. It will also be useful to Chief Executives and senior management personnel who have a key role in managing fundraising programmes.

I have worked at senior level for fifteen years in the not for profit world and fundraising was always my principal issue. Why? Because fundraising is a survival issue for not for profits. No matter how worthy your work, if you can't persuade people to support you financially, you will close. I refer in this book to 'not for profits' because this book is written not just for people in the traditional charities or voluntary bodies, but for a much broader constituency. You will find this book useful if you work in a hospital, church group, school or community group. Today, a great diversity of groups are turning to fundraising in order to survive. Wherever you work, if you are involved in fundraising this book has something for you.

When I started to write *A Practical Guide to Fundraising and Public Relations* I set out to give clear and practical help to anyone contemplating raising funds. My goal was to provide the reader with an easy-to-use and practical approach to fundraising – something I would have valued in my work.

I firmly believe that the fundamental interdependence of fundraising and public relations cannot be overstated. I discuss this in chapter 1. When you want to give practical effect to this you will find all you need to get your basic PR kit ready in chapter 15.

In order to allow you to dip into the relevant sections to obtain specific information I have divided the *Guide* into three parts:

Part 1. Understand the basic components of fundraising
Part 2. Use these six successful ways to fundraise
Part 3. Get down to it – your plans and your PR kit

In Part 1 the importance of planning is emphasised. The four chapters will give you a good grounding in the basics of planning. When you have studied them you can go on to produce your own plans using the formats in chapter 16.

In my experience – and that of the many fundraisers I have worked with – two groups are crucial to your success as a fundraiser: volunteers and donors. I have seen many good fundraisers burn out from sheer exhaustion because of inadequate backup. I can't overemphasise the need to build a network of volunteers who will help you. For this reason I have put together an eight-point programme for a successful volunteer programme.

It may seem obvious that donors are important, so why then do we take them for granted? Donor recognition, or saying thank you, is so important that I have devoted the whole of chapter 6 to it.

In Part 2, six very practical chapters offer clear, concise approaches to tried-and-tested approaches to fundraising. I have been involved in all of these and my advice comes from the lessons of hard experience.

Part 3 will enable you to write your own plans and prepare your PR kit. It is always good to keep up with the latest developments, so please refer to the resources section, which will give you useful reading references and contact names and addresses.

This book is about getting results when you fundraise. It will equip you in planning to succeed and will give you a clear and concise outlook. I hope that you will find this book a useful resource to dip into as you begin your fundraising career, or a refresher for those of you well down the fundraising road.

My associates and I are very interested in hearing from anyone involved in fundraising. Please contact us at our address listed in the resources section.

Finally, I would like to wish you the best of luck in your fundraising career.

Veronica Canning
March 1999

1

FUNDRAISING AND PUBLIC RELATIONS ARE INTEGRATED

Introduction

This is a book of ideas, not 'iron-clad' answers. There are no sure-fire formulas, but there are ideas and practical tools that can be taken by management and staff and applied to their organisations and to their own working styles. It is based on my fifteen years' experience learning the hard way by working in fundraising and public relations. The most important conclusion I have come to is that working as a fundraiser is no different from working in a commercial business. Both demand results. To succeed in both, you must be clearly focused, plan strategically and continually evaluate.

But before we explore the fundraising world, it is important to look at the larger world of the voluntary sector.

The importance of the voluntary sector

A report, *Dimensions of the Voluntary Sector*, states that in the United Kingdom the total income of the top 500 charities was estimated at almost £3.7 billion in 1995/96. It provides one in 25 full-time jobs and the value of unpaid contributions by volunteers is around £25 billion.

One of the distinguishing features of the voluntary sector is the variety of groups that the not for profit organisation serves – beneficiaries or clients, the general public, donors, volunteers, board members. Consider also that the not for profits are serving all of them simultaneously. Both fundraisers and PR practitioners are crucial to the organisation's service of these different groups. Further complications arise for fundraisers and PR people alike in that the lines are blurred between these groups.

Beneficiaries can become donors, who also volunteer. A mother of a child with juvenile arthritis, who has attended support group sessions for parents of a child with a chronic illness, is a beneficiary. She may be so appreciative of the help she and her family receive that she will become a regular donor.

As her child gets older and the whole family learns to cope, she may volunteer to help with the support group for parents who have just learnt that their child has arthritis. She is a beneficiary, a donor and a volunteer.

Today, with the Charity Commissions' register listing about 180,000 charities in England and Wales alone, lifelong loyalty to any one voluntary organisation can no longer be taken for granted. People have a vast choice of worthy causes all asking for their time and their money so they may migrate from cause to cause. The challenge for both PR and fundraising is to keep people committed to your organisation. The costs of acquiring new donors and volunteers are too high not to invest in ways of retaining the ones you already have.

Our world is changing

There have been remarkable changes in the not for profit world in the last ten years. Today, we face economic, social and governmental change as never before. Fundraising, as a core function, is being forced to adapt to these changes. Good public relations is needed as never before. Why?

☐ Fundraising is highly competitive, with increasing numbers of voluntary organisations in search of scarce funds. The market is crowded, so your public relations must mark you out and ensure that your organisation connects with people.

☐ Greater sophistication in the media and of donors has challenged fundraisers to improve their methods of communication. Well-planned public relations is essential today.

☐ The realisation that voluntary giving is such a key source of income and that income from that source is levelling off has made the role of direct mail and database fundraising crucial. The messages being sent by direct mail must come under the overall PR umbrella of your organisation or you will end up sending mixed signals.

☐ The increase in the number of not for profits is a real consideration. Greater planning and focus, in all aspects of fundraising and public relations, are needed not just to compete but to survive.

☐ It is possible for a fundraiser or PR practitioner to be successful in a quickly changing voluntary sector. This book explains how to plan your way to success and provides valuable practical skills to make your plan a reality.

Fundraising and public relations

What is fundraising?

Fundraising is largely about persuading people to part with their hard-earned money. You are asking them to write you a cheque, put cash in a box, make you a covenant, attend your function or – amazingly – leave you money in their will.

What is public relations?

It is important to remember that all organisations have public relations, whether they do anything about it or not. Public relations is not something you can switch on and off; it is there all the time. Your organisation has a public image – good, bad or indifferent. Unfortunately, passive PR can be harmful as you have no control over what message is being received by the groups you are targeting. Nature abhors a vacuum and so every vacuum is filled. Consequently, it is better to make your own PR rather than let others do it for you. The challenge to the fundraiser is to ensure that the organisation projects a positive image.

Fundraising and public relations

Fundraising without public relations is like Romeo without Juliet: it is only one half of the equation. My experience of fundraising over the past fifteen years has convinced me that not only is fundraising without excellent PR backup exhausting, disappointing and frustrating, it is financially unproductive.

Think about it. Would you give money to someone you don't know? No, of course not. You might give a pound or two, but nothing more. Conducting your fundraising in a vacuum, where no one knows about you, is the same as asking a stranger for money. It gets the same negative results.

At the most elementary level, to fundraise successfully you have to let people know who you are and what you do.

Four likely attitudes people may have to your organisation and what your public relations response should be:

1. They may be blissfully unaware of your existence.

That's not as bad as it seems at first. People with a negative viewpoint, as we discuss later, are far more difficult to handle. When people are unaware of you this gives you a free hand. You can choose your PR strategy. When you have read this book you'll know whom to target and with what message to get effective results.

2. They may know a little about you and want to know more.

These are positive people. They will respond to targeted messages. They will ask questions and decide whether to give, depending on the answer. This is when a well thought-out PR strategy covering all communications from your organisation pays off.

3. They are hostile to you.

This is the most difficult group. They are the lethal because not only do they not donate, but they can also stop others donating. Your public relations is most challenged by this group because you have to do two things – overcome the negativity and then replace it with a positive attitude.

4. They know you and they have already donated.

It is easy to become complacent about this group. After all, they may be giving money regularly. You might think you have bigger mountains to climb – like getting that major donor you've been pursuing for the last year. More than any other group, they need a thought-out PR strategy. You must keep them informed about what you do with their money. You must make them feel included and, above all, appreciated. Your PR and donor recognition policies must interact.

People give money to organisations they perceive to be doing a useful and worthwhile job. Public relations is a vital way of ensuring your potential donor knows what a good job you are doing. A useful strategy for planning a PR programme is to highlight the problem or need you are focusing on, and then position the charity in the public eye as responding to that need. For example, a health-related not for profit may hold an awareness day when they highlight the extent of the health problem using statistics and case histories. Then, they hold a major fundraising campaign soon afterwards to capitalise on the heightened awareness.

Always seek publicity for your fundraising projects. No matter how small the project, if it is presented in an interesting and useful way to the media, there is a chance that they will give it some coverage.

There is a growing realisation that fundraisers need to be sure that potential donors know the exact purpose of the organisation, how it works, its financial viability and how the money collected is spent. With increased competition among organisations for funds, fundraisers cannot afford to be complacent about keeping donors informed. Effective fundraising results send out your message on two levels: general information about what your organisation does, and focused fundraising publicity information about your organisation to prospective donors.

In smaller not for profits the fundraising and PR function can be combined. In this instance, you can have a direct influence on what is happening. In larger organisations, where they are in separate departments, it is vital that the fundraising people develop close links with the PR staff. Public relations can continue without a fundraising input, but not the other way round. So the onus is on the fundraisers to establish and maintain good relationships.

Chapter 10 gives you your basic PR kit, detailing what you need to produce a press release, a press pack and a press contact list. It also advises you on PR events, including press conferences, photo-opportunities and effective participation in exhibitions.

Taking stock in a rapidly changing world

Before embarking on any major fundraising or PR planning it is essential that you analyse exactly what is happening now. Chapter 3 gives you the tools to do this. You must put your fundraising and PR activities under the microscope. You should look at each fundraising activity and decide whether it is a winner or not, and you should look at what part your public relations played.

All not for profits are witnessing the remarkable changes that have taken place in the last decade. What distinguishes successful ones is their ability to change and navigate through the change. The hallmarks of success are:

☐ Keeping up with changing trends both in charitable giving and in PR communication.
☐ Self-awareness – produced by realistic evaluation of the organisation's programmes, including the fundraising and PR ones.
☐ Planning in all aspects of the organisation's work – involving setting objectives and a focus on achieving them.
☐ Knowing the environment in which you are operating.

Chapters 2, 3 and 4 offer practical advice on writing focused, results-oriented plans.

Is your public relations helping you listen?

Gone are the days when not for profits were set up to deliver a service or fill a need and, twenty years later, were still there – still working along the same lines. Now, voluntary organisations must listen to a variety of groups, from donors to beneficiaries, and adapt to meet their changing needs. Fundraising strategies must be built around what people want, not what the organisation wants.

How do fundraisers and public relations staff deliver a range of appropriate products to their varied target groups? Well, first they evaluate what they are doing now, find out what their target group wants, decide their objectives and design a strategy to deliver them. In short, they engage in a *planned approach to their work*. The next four chapters of this book will equip you to do this.

As a fundraiser you quickly learn the need to discover your donors' interest and satisfy it. Quizzing and listening to donors is crucial to all fundraising. Your organisation has some interests also. Good fundraising satisfies both interests simultaneously.

Is your public relations getting you fundraising volunteers?

Volunteers are crucial to the success of fundraising, and public relations is an important tool for their recruitment. Through your PR programme you will have built up a high profile in the community so when you ask for help, people will be positively aware of your organisation.

Volunteers exchange their time or money for something else, because they perceive what they are receiving to be of greater value. For example, a senior executive in a company serves on a fundraising committee and gives up his time. In return, he receives the enhanced status of being associated with a well-known and prestigious not for profit organisation and of visibly serving his community. In short, your public relations must project an organisation with which volunteers want to be associated.

The realities: fundraising trends

Fundraising is one of the most difficult activities anyone can undertake. To be a successful fundraiser you have to undertake a wide range of activities. Frequently, fundraisers are described as persuasive, charming people – they are that, but more fundamentally, very successful fundraisers are clear thinkers, people with a vision, who can see what they want and how they are going to get there. They are, above all, highly practical and know when to go with a project and when to walk away from it.

Because so many of the very good fundraisers I've worked with valued practicalities above 'exciting ideas', I've made this book very practical. It covers the broad spectrum of fundraising techniques from special events through direct mail to applying for grants.

Given that fundraising is crucial to the very survival of many not for profits and that public relations is a key support function, what then of the 'fundraising environment' in which you will be operating? In this regard it is useful to take a brief look at the latest trends. For this I'm grateful to a number of sources but most especially to *Dimensions of the Voluntary Sector* (1997) from Charities Aid Foundation (CAF), from which the following figures are drawn.

Total income

In 1996 the total income of Charities Aid Foundation's top 500 charities was £3.7 billion. For them total income in real terms declined by 1 per cent.

Voluntary income

Voluntary income is a crucial element of most not for profits' income. In fact, half the income of CAF's top 500 fundraising charities is dependent on voluntary public support. The worrying point is that the level of income from this source has become static and CAF says growth is declining in the long term. Voluntary income to CAF's top 500 fundraising charities grew by just 1 per cent in real terms in 1996. The slowdown in the growth rate was due mainly to a real-term decline in legacy income of 3.4 per cent.

Much of chapter 7 on techniques of fundraising concentrates on the different aspects of voluntary fundraising because it is such an important source of income. Chapters 5 and 9 give practical pointers to knowing your donors and improving your donor recognition techniques.

Grant-making trusts

There is a total of 8,793 charitable grant-makers in the UK with a total of £1,854 million in funds available. Their investment income is increasing and so CAF's top 500 grant-making trusts are increasing the funds available. The National Lottery has increased funds from this source. They gave grants totalling £478 million in 1995 and 1996.

At first glance this seems a bewildering array of organisations to sort through. The section on grants in chapter 7 will equip you to make an effective approach and gives information on all the other sources of help available.

Corporate donors

According to *Dimensions of the Voluntary Sector* (1997), the total figure for corporate cash donations is £262 million. Total cash donations by CAF's top 500 corporate donors increased by 9 per cent between 1994/95 and 1995/96. However, resources from this group to the voluntary sector have not peaked. Fundraisers can profitably target this area for increased income. Chapter 7 will help you raise funds for your organisation from corporate donors.

Many small voluntary organisations can learn from the sections on building relationships with donors and running professional events. However, because of their small size, they have special considerations. These are also discussed in the section of chapter 7 dealing with local fundraising.

Part 1

UNDERSTAND THE BASIC COMPONENTS OF FUNDRAISING

Vital to fundraising but often hidden from view is the slow and detailed planning that precedes and follows all fundraising and PR activities.

Part 1 of this book introduces you to planning (chapter 2) and takes you through the stages of planning from getting a clear overview (chapter 3) to setting goals (chapter 4) and finally to evaluating your results (chapter 5).

Two groups of people are crucial to fundraising success – donors and volunteers. Chapter 6 will help you source donors, increase your understanding of them and help you ensure their continued support through excellent donor recognition. Chapter 7 outlines an eight-step approach to building a successful volunteer programme. If the constraints to fundraising are to be overcome they must be recognised. Chapter 7 begins this process.

2

PLANNING FOR RESULTS: THE KEY TO SUCCESSFUL FUNDRAISING

Introduction

This chapter demonstrates the need for planning in order to achieve good fundraising and PR results. It demonstrates that every fundraiser must plan for successful results by taking control of the fundraising process or risk lurching from project to project, using up staff and volunteer time and not getting the maximum return for the effort invested.

Planning for a fundraising or public relations department is no different from planning for an overall organisation. The same clarity and detailed work are involved. However, it is important when embarking on your fundraising or PR plan to be very familiar with the organisation's overall plan, if one exists.

What is planning?

Planning means clarifying what it is you want to do, the purpose for doing it and deciding on clear steps to achieve it. Deciding within what period you want results is another key element.

Both fundraising and public relations lend themselves to planning. Results and clarity of purpose can be greatly enhanced when a planning process is undertaken. A good plan means going through a number of stages. These are outlined later in the chapter.

First let us look at nine good reasons why planning will help you.

Nine good reasons why fundraisers must plan

1. Asking too often offends!

It may seem very obvious but *people donate money*. Even in big corporations it is usually down to one person to say yes or no. Therefore, fundraisers must

Table 2.1 Seven reasons to make planning an integral part of your work

1. If you don't plan you will always be focused on the present. You will work for the immediate future and only have a short-term view.
2. Planning enables you to set goals and have something to work towards.
3. Planning lets you see the whole picture – you can have an overview of your work and what is required of you.
4. A plan helps you keep on track. You can always return to your plan after an unexpected event or period of intense work. It helps you to refocus.
5. If you don't know what you set out to do, how do you know if you have achieved it? A plan can be reviewed and you can see if your original objectives have been met or not.
6. Planning has to be done against time deadlines – therefore you become aware of the need for planning use of your time. Good time management is an essential ally of planning.
7. A good plan enables you to remain focused on the priorities of your job despite the many conflicting pressures put on you by the many bosses in NGOs like committee members, volunteers, the public, pressure groups or other staff.

not turn people off. Asking people for money in an unplanned way is guaranteed to annoy them. A common mistake is to ask too often for the same cause. Just because a donor came to your film première in February, doesn't mean you should ask them to a golf classic in July *and* a gala dinner in October.

A good plan formulated in advance with specifically targeted sectors will help eliminate this problem. Too many events too close together run by an unresourced fundraising office can result in shortcuts being made. It is easier to keep using the same lists rather than take time to research new ones. Eventually, these donors will become fed up and stop giving altogether.

2. Fundraising can burn out staff and volunteers

Fundraising, especially hands-on events, demands masses of energy. Unlike direct mail campaigns which can be run from a desk, gala dinners, flag days, golf classics and other high-profile events demand that staff and volunteers have to get out and sell. Volunteers are giving up their free time to come to help your organisation, so you must not be unreasonable in your demands.

Staff get physically and mentally tired if asked to go from one big event to another. No matter how dedicated people are, you will lose their support if having worked all week, they are also expected to give up their evenings and every weekend.

If you plan events and fundraising jobs in advance, then volunteers can be asked to help with a limited number of events only spread across the year. People appreciate this and will stay involved. This is a long-term investment which will allow you to build up a group of people who will help with certain favourite activities.

3. Fundraising events have long lead-in times

Almost all fundraising activities have long lead-in times – be it getting the permit for a street collection or booking a celebrity for a fundraising concert. In prestige events, increased competition between not for profits vying for the same market has seen standards rise. People now expect good value for money *and* to be well looked after. To pull this off, the event must be very well organised and great attention paid to detail.

Approaching people for money by phone or mail requires meticulous planning to avoid duplication and wastage. Materials must be designed, approved, printed and posted. Ample time is required in case any problems arise. A mail shot in August could take up to six months' advance work. If you don't take a long-range view, then the stages will be carried out under intense pressure and mistakes made – mistakes which ultimately cost money.

4. Fundraisers have to avoid clashing with other similar or competing events

A well-planned and innovative fundraising campaign can be ruined because it clashes with a similar event. If you are having a golf classic and stage it on the same day as the Ryder Cup, your target market won't come. Holding your street collection on the same day as Red Nose day is a mistake – you'll end up in a David and Goliath contest and lose!

When drawing up your fundraising plan find out when major national holidays, cultural and sporting events are taking place and work round them.

5. Plan for obsolescence

Fundraising is subject to trends like all other aspects of selling and marketing. Think of a fundraising project as if it were a product. You can expect it to go through a product cycle – sales build to a peak, reach a plateau, begin to decline, first slowly and then quickly to the end. You will find more information on the product cycle in chapter 7.

If you know this, you can plan to start one project when another is at its peak. This can be a difficult concept to sell to voluntary organisations and their committees. If something is going well, they may think it will go on like that forever – but if it fails, they may think the fundraiser has done something wrong. Good planning shows that the fundraiser is aware of these cycles.

6. Don't neglect the bread-and-butter fundraisers

Fundraisers can be dazzled by the large and exciting events in their calendar. However, small-scale annual events together can often make up a sizeable percentage of your income. It is easy to become complacent about them. Each one, no matter how small, is an important contributor. Never take them for granted – fundraising events, especially successful ones, are hard to replace.

When drawing up your annual plan, time can be allotted to meet the people involved and to ensure that they feel appreciated. Schedule smaller events for slacker times so that they will not be overlooked.

7. Remember to allow for the unexpected

One of the hallmarks of fundraising is the constant surprises it brings. You may be approached by someone with a good fundraising idea at any time. Sponsors often come forward after they have seen your organisation run a good event. Success can lead to more success, so you must build time into your plan to take advantage of this kind of development. If you have a good plan, you will appear well organised and coherent to unexpected approaches. And you can turn them to your advantage by inviting the would-be sponsor to join an event planned for later in the year.

8. Leave time to think

Fundraisers are so busy going from one fundraising project to the next that they often forget to take time out to think. Thoughtful assessment and learning from mistakes are overlooked. Many fundraisers laugh at the idea of taking a day out to think. They may not realise it, but that day – especially if it's spent with a 'think-in' group – could make them more money in the long run.

You should plan to take one day each quarter for time to assess what has just happened and to plan the next twelve months. Spend time with the people directly involved in fundraising and assess the current situation. Once a year it is a good idea to assemble a group of creative people – actors, writers, public relations, advertising and marketing people – for a brainstorming session. It is amazing what ideas can be generated. It is a renewing experience for a jaded fundraiser.

9. Planning eliminates budget overruns

It is impossible to organise any fundraising activities without being completely taken up by the cost of everything and the need not to waste money. If you go too far down that road, you can lose sight of the overall picture. A plan of fundraising projects showing expected net income after costs can give a realistic overview. All fundraising ventures are risky – they can fail to make money and, in a worst-case scenario, lose money. Every fundraiser will try something innovative each year to ensure that new projects are coming on stream to replace fundraising ventures that are coming to the end of their life. An annual plan will ensure that you don't embark on too many of these in one year and that they are spaced between reliable earners.

Planning should involve all interested parties

All successful plans are dependent on a wide variety of people. You can conceive the plan by yourself and make a very good job of it, but getting things done requires others. This is particularly true of not for profits where so much work is expected of a small number of staff and volunteers.

When you have mapped out your draft annual plan you should meet a range of other people to get their views. Find out what their year looks like and build their busy and slack periods into your plan. If administration staff are less busy in the summer, that would be the time to ask for help with inputting prospect names on to a database for a forthcoming gala dinner.

If you're are running fundraising and someone else is handling public relations, your plans should be co-ordinated closely because they are interrelated and you don't want to be looking for volunteers to help with a national flag day when the PR people are looking for volunteers for a lobbying campaign.

If one committee or board member is closely allied to a particular fundraising drive like direct mail or heading up a fundraising committee, it is essential to build that project around their diary. If not, you risk losing their involvement and support.

Likely stakeholders
- [ ] Chief Executive
- [ ] Board
- [ ] Support fundraising staff
- [ ] Heads of other departments.
  Public Relations
  Volunteer Programme
  Services
  Administration
- [ ] Clients/customers
- [ ] Local branches and committees around the country.

Involve your co-workers

It may be clear to you why a good plan is essential to your fundraising and public relations, but do make sure you involve your co-workers. They may not realise how important planning is. They may be too involved in their own activities to take any notice of what you are doing. That's fair enough if you operate in separate spheres, but if you need their co-operation to implement some aspect of your plan, and they don't feel that you have consulted and involved them, they can scupper the whole project by not co-operating.

Imagine you need to have people to staff a large stand at a major exhibition. You have made all the arrangements, organised the artwork, got budgets approved and on Friday evening you ask the volunteer organiser to round up nine people for the next day. More than likely they won't. They will be unwilling to appear so 'last minute' and, anyway, the volunteers may be involved in another project. If you'd involved that person earlier and asked their advice on using volunteers in your fundraising and PR activities, they would be on your side. They might even have reminded you about it.

Planning is a guide – not something carved in stone

Remember that the 'plan' is a useful tool or guide to help you achieve what you have set out to do. It is a tool, not an inflexible code – it is not meant to put you in a straitjacket.

It is important to be practical, especially in the area of public relations and fundraising in not for profits. It is a very changeable and uncertain area and so this must always be in the back of your mind. Allowances must be made for the unexpected because no two days in the fundraising department of a not for profits are the same.

Planning – a staged process

Different planners use different stages and call them different names. A quick look at Table 2.2 will demystify them for you.

Essentially, writing a plan is a voyage of discovery. First, you have to be very clear about what you are supposed to be doing – the *purpose of your job*. It helps if you also check on the purpose of the not for profit employer, to ensure that there is no conflict.

You will have heard of *mission statements* and it is useful to have one for your job.

Before deciding what you are going to do in your plan you must *analyse the existing situation* and collect as much information as you can. Chapter 3 will guide you through that process.

Next, identify the *strategic decisions* that have to be made. You now begin to realise that you will have to say no to some things in order to achieve others. A sense of direction and a strategy begins to emerge. We shall look at this in chapter 4 and see how to turn your strategy into a set of *achievable objectives*.

Table 2.2 Know the language of planning

Vision
The vision states what the organisation aspires to be. It tells you why this organisation was established originally and why it continues now.

Mission
The mission defines the organisation's purpose and goals. It is often expressed in a mission statement.

Objectives
These are the detailed goals, often laid out in work plans, which guide the work of the organisation in reaching its goals.

The cold reality of *budgeting* then intervenes and you have to decide what you can afford to do. This is a key part of planning in not for profits where so many decisions are made against a background of financial insecurity.

An integral part of any plan is *evaluation*: chapter 12 will help you evaluate your plans.

Six negative views of planning in not for profits

Your role as a fundraiser or PR person is heavily influenced by the mindset of the not for profit in which you work. You must take the ethos and mentality of the founders, board members and senior staff into account. Fundraising and PR staff need to interact with *all* the people in the organisation.

Why planning is important to public relations!

It is important to remember that all organisations have public relations whether they do anything about it or not. Unfortunately, passive PR can be harmful as it means you have no control over the message that your public is getting about you. Far better to make your own PR than have others do it for you!

Good public relations is based on a well thought-out strategic plan.

The Catholic Agency CAFOD was reported in *Charity* magazine to be completely revamping its fundraising strategy in an attempt to widen its supporter base. It intends to achieve a planned and focused approach to fundraising by revolving all its fundraising efforts around a single theme. The themes chosen for three years are: healthcare in 1998, education in 1999 and food in 2000.

Setting overall goals for your organisation's programmes greatly assists

Table 2.3 Six negative views of planning in not for profits

1. **The Amateur is Best Syndrome**
   A small organisation run largely by people who were once volunteers but are now paid staff. They have kept their pioneer/volunteer approach and reject any formalisation of work. They don't like targets, deadlines, prioritisation or saying no. Planning can cramp their style.

2. **The Help Me Syndrome**
   One-issue organisations – like single-illness groups – tend to focus on what the organisation is doing for them. Unfortunately, not everyone has the same idea of what is needed, so factions occur. Getting a consensus for a plan can be difficult.

3. **The Help Everyone Syndrome**
   Emergency response charities – particularly in the third world sector – like to respond to high-profile emergencies. Problems of planning arise when multiple catastrophes occur at the same time.

4. **The Messiah Syndrome**
   Issue-led charities which rely on lobbying and protests. Planning can be a problem as it requires cool rationale and sensitivity. These charities are run by people with passionate views. They are in many ways the public face of the organisation. You need to understand them fully. No one organisation can be totally characterised as one type, however certain syndromes exist. Have a look at these and see if they fit your organisation or any section of it. It will comfort you to know that you are not facing challenges unique to you.

5. **The Volunteer Knows Best Syndrome**
   Many not for profits are run by professional staff with fundraising and public relations people, but they are closely shadowed by a group of volunteers who second them on every little question/detail. These volunteers really don't want staff to have any power or authority. They want to keep all authority to voluntary committees. Staff find themselves with responsibility but without authority. Planning in this instance can be fraught unless the volunteers really agree with plans.

6. **The Only I Know What Our Clients Need Syndrome**
   Staff who work for a long time in a not for profits can succumb to this. In third world charities staff officers in charge of regions can often be heard speaking of the needs of 'their people'. In health-related charities, particularly involving disability, staff can speak on behalf of people without asking what they feel. This is the worst aspect of 'Does he take sugar?' approach. Planning here requires listening a lot and clearly involving these staff. If they think you might harm the interests of the people they represent, they will not work with you and they might even sabotage your PR or fundraising efforts.

the fundraiser in setting fundraising goals. Obviously, when you know what you are planning to do it is easier to approach donors.

The Marie Curie Cancer Organisation launched a new strategy to widen its services to include more full-time nurses and extend research facilities.

The plans were set out in its *Strategy for the Millennium* document, which charts its plans for the next five years. This document will be used when approaching statutory and charitable funders, according to their Chief Executive.

Seven tips to using your time productively as a fundraiser

1. Target the major donor

In some not for profits up to 90 per cent of funds can come from as little as 1 per cent of the donor base. In general though, remember the 80:20 rule – 20 per cent of donors give 80 per cent of the money – so use your time accordingly. Spend more time on your major donors.

2. Try to turn your small donations into pledges over a number of years

It is very hard work starting afresh each year, looking for small donations from the same people. Try to get loyal but small donors to commit themselves over a number of years. It makes for better and more productive use of your time.

3. Think before you leap

An hour spent in fundraising planning can save you four hours in fundraising activity. In planning, you decide what you want to achieve in five years' time and you work back to your yearly, monthly, weekly and finally to your daily plan.

4. Prioritise – but be realistic about what you can achieve

Prioritise your time in line with your fundraising targets. If setting up your direct mail campaign is your priority for the next three months, so be it. However, be certain that you can do this in three months because, if it normally takes six months, you'll be lining yourself up for stress and failure.

5. Don't rush into asking for money

Learning about your donors and educating them about your organisation is a good use of a fundraiser's time. When the time comes to ask for a donation you will find that your preparation work has paid off.

6. New donors like new customers are expensive to find

So make sure you spend time looking after your existing ones. Time spent thanking donors is crucial. Never approach someone for a donation until you have thanked them for their last one. A useful rule of thumb is – the more they give the more you thank them. A major donor should receive at least six messages of thanks and recognition before being approached again. These can range from a personal letter from the Chief Executive to a dinner with the president, through to an invitation to a major event like a gala dinner or film première

7. Don't get swallowed up in special events

Be careful about special events. They can completely take over a fundraiser's life, leaving no time to think, plan or build long-term fundraising initiatives.

While excellent in themselves, from a fundraising and PR point of view, the thing to control is the number each year.

Summary points

1. Before you begin the planning process learn the vocabulary and the stages of a plan.
2. Involve all the interested parties or stakeholders in the planning process.
3. There are nine good reasons to convince you that you need planning to carry out your fundraising and public relations work.
4. Be familiar with the objections to planning found in voluntary organisations.
5. Use the seven tips to improve your productivity as a fundraiser.

3

GETTING A CLEAR OVERVIEW: ANALYSE EXISTING FUNDRAISING AND PUBLIC RELATIONS

Introduction

This chapter takes you through four stages of getting a clear overview of your fundraising or PR activities.

The first stage for a newly appointed fundraiser or experienced fundraiser reviewing a fundraising programme must be to take an overview of existing activities. This chapter will give the practical tools to do this and guide you through the process. When you have finished reading this chapter, you should turn to chapter 16 where these tools are reproduced so that you can carry out your own analysis. An easy-to-use format for surveying existing activities is provided.

Second, this chapter introduces you to a range of analytical tools for use when you examine your existing fundraising or PR activities. SWOT analysis and portfolio analysis are explained. It is vital to assess the current situation in public relations or fundraising as this will affect the best choice of a strategy for the future.

In the third stage you assess whether you are achieving the maximum in your most favoured activities. The product cycle and Pareto principle are outlined and their relevance explained.

Define the present strategy

The secret of success is to be ready for opportunity when it comes.

– Disraeli

In order to evaluate how well your present fundraising or PR strategy is working, it is vital to identify what that strategy is.

The most important element of a fundraising strategy is how you are trying to compete. Is your strategy to differentiate your not for profit from your rivals by having only local-level fundraising or focusing exclusively on one major fundraising drive a year? Is the PR strategy to focus narrowly on a specific range of groups and not try to reach the wider public?

Fundraising and public relations do not operate in isolation. The present strategy is underpinned by other support functions in the organisation such as marketing, education and social programmes, finance, and human resources, both professional and voluntary. These need to be identified and understood.

The organisation may have recently begun a particular drive or launched a PR campaign because of external factors like threatened cuts of government grants.

It is not enough to identify different parts of the fundraising or PR strategy; you need to understand what the rationale is for each piece of the strategy. To analyse the situation fully you must see how the different parts of the fundraising or PR strategy fit together.

It is relatively easy to map out and analyse past successes and failures. What is not so obvious, but is crucial to success, is to figure how well the present strategy is related to the expected future sector and competitors' environment.

Your key considerations include:

☐ Does the present strategy respond to the sector's driving forces and the strategic issues confronting the sector?
☐ How well does the present strategy take into account the future key success factors?
☐ How much has the present strategy taken into account future adverse factors?
☐ Are the organisation's support resources adequate for the road ahead?

Step 1: Getting a financial overview

As your success as a fundraiser is dependent on income earned and reaching targets, it is a good idea to base all planning on a clear financial overview of the organisation. You therefore need to know all sources of income and their relative importance.

What are the main sources of income?

Speak to the Director, financial controller, accountant or chairperson of the finance committee. Get lists of all incoming money. Get a copy of the audited accounts for the last five years. The purpose of doing all this research is to have the information you need to compile an analysis chart of all income. The chart you are going to construct will look like Table 3.1.

You now know which fundraising activities generate most income, their

Table 3.1 Survey of existing income

Source of Income Last Year	Amount £	% Total Income	Amount Last Year £	Change
Direct Mail Campaigns				
1.				
2.				
3.				
4.				
Major Gifts				
Workplace Giving				
Covenants				
Bequests				
Special Events				
☐ Large-scale				
1.				
2.				
3.				
4.				
☐ Small-scale Total				
Grants				
Government				
1.				
2.				
3.				
4.				

Foundations/Trusts
1.
2.
3.
4.
Corporate Donations
1.
2.
3.
4.
Sponsorship
1.
2.
3.
TOTALS

relative importance in overall income-generating activities and whether they have increased this year over last year.

How have they performed in the last five years?

Now, you need to get a profile of the major earners' performance over the last five years. This will help you decide their position in the product cycle. (The product cycle is discussed in greater detail later in this chapter.)

Step 2: Using tools of analysis

After you have taken the important first step of analysing the financial situation you can move on to the next stage and take a fundamental look at all your fundraising or PR activities. A number of different analytical tools will help you and include:

Table 3.2 Survey of income over last five years

Source of Income	Year 1 (%)	Year 2 (%)	Year 3 (%)	Year 4 (%)
Voluntary Income				
Direct Mail Campaigns				
1.				
2.				
3.				
4.				
Major Gifts				
Workplace Giving				
Covenants				
Bequests				
Special Events				
☐ Large-scale				
1.				
2.				
3.				
4.				
☐ Small-scale Total				
Grants				
Government				
1.				
2.				

3.

4.

Foundations/Trusts

1.

2.

3.

4.

Corporate Donations

1.

2.

3.

4.

Sponsorship

1.

2.

3.

TOTALS

A SWOT analysis

SWOT is an acronym for Strengths, Weaknesses, Opportunities and Threats – an appraisal of your fundraising and public relations' internal Strengths and Weaknesses, market Opportunities and external Threats.

It can be useful to think of strengths and weaknesses as being in the present and threats and opportunities as being in the future, or about to happen. A SWOT analysis examines the internal strengths and weaknesses and the external opportunities and threats. It is an easy-to-use tool for getting an overview of your organisation's or department's strategic situation.

Carrying out a SWOT analysis introduces the fundamental link between the internal processes and the external situation represented by threats and opportunities.

Identifying strengths and weaknesses

Not surprisingly a strength is something an organisation or department is good at doing, or a characteristic that gives it an important capability. You will see it can be a skill, competent and experienced personnel or even good ideas.

A weakness is something an organisation or department does badly or lacks. It could be poorly trained staff or lack of financial control.

Some common strengths and weaknesses are listed in Figures 3.1 and 3.2. Remember: we all find it easier to list negatives than positives. You'll find the list of weaknesses and threats fills up quickly, but do pay equal attention to the strengths and opportunities.

Once you have carried out this exercise you have to evaluate your lists very carefully. Some strengths are more important than others because they affect your performance and ability to compete successfully. Likewise, some weaknesses can be potentially fatal, unlike others which can be easily rectified.

It is worth considering building your strategy and plans on your strongest attributes, be they staff, skills or innovative products. A good strategy should build on strengths while eliminating weaknesses that make the organisation or department vulnerable.

Identifying opportunities and threats

New opportunities can only be acted on if the organisation or department is ready and geared up to respond. Care has to be taken not to destabilise existing programmes and activities by devoting all resources to one new opportunity.

Unless you are ready to pursue an opportunity and unless it is really relevant and fits in with your overall plan it could make more sense not to respond.

There is a difference between opportunities for your particular not for profit and the not for profit sector in general. Certain organisations are well placed to exploit opportunities, but it is no good berating yourself for a lost opportunity – you might not have been able to respond well anyway.

External threats may come from your competitors, changes in your donor base or shifting media interests. Identifying threats is important, not only because of their potential adverse effect on the organisation, but also because they can undermine your overall strategy.

Internal Strengths	External Opportunities
☐ Special competence of staff or volunteers ☐ Well thought of by media ☐ Well connected to media ☐ An acknowledged excellence in public relations ☐ Well thought-out PR strategy ☐ A history of good public relations campaigns ☐ Good at getting public relations from every aspect of the organisation's programme ☐ Innovative ideas ☐ Experienced staff good at getting coverage on low budget	☐ Broad media interest in your sector could be focused on your organisation ☐ Become media 'expert' called on for comment. ☐ Add new target groups ☐ Adopt totally new strategy to match changed circumstances ☐ Complacency among rival organisations in your interest area ☐ New radio and TV station, new publications ☐ Expand public relations activities to meet broader range of interests of different age groups
Internal Weaknesses	**External Threats**
☐ No clear strategy ☐ No plans ☐ *Ad hoc* approach ☐ Lack of co-operation between staff and volunteers ☐ Lack of liaison between internal departments in organisation ☐ Public relations department does not know what other departments are doing ☐ Lack of management capability ☐ Missing key skills ☐ Poor track record ☐ Poor financial control ☐ No innovation ☐ Failure by senior management to properly resource public relations	☐ Likely experience of new but similar organisations ☐ Competitive forces ☐ Other similar organisations taking the spotlight ☐ Slow down in interest in your organisation ☐ Failure to reassess organisation's services and loss of people to more relevant organisations ☐ Changes in public opinion

Figure 3.1 SWOT analysis: public relations

If your strategy is to succeed, it must combine maximising opportunities best suited to the organisation with defending it against external threats.

Common points to look for:

Internal Strengths	External Opportunities
☐ Competent staff ☐ Good volunteer involvement ☐ Good record of innovation ☐ Ability to replace ageing products with new ones ☐ Good cost control ☐ Well connected to industry and media ☐ Good record on delivering value for money ☐ Good donor appreciation programme ☐ Good strategic plan ☐ Good at planning for medium to long term	☐ New media interest in your speciality ☐ Introduction of new service opens up new market sector ☐ Special anniversary or year, e.g., 'Year of Disabled' ☐ New funds available from government or EU ☐ New legislation ☐ Local or world events ☐ Big sporting events
Internal Weaknesses	**External Threats**
☐ Lack of staff ☐ Lack of volunteers ☐ High turnover of staff and volunteers ☐ Burn-out common in personnel ☐ Lack of innovation ☐ Failure to replace fundraising products before they expire ☐ Lack of cost control ☐ *Ad hoc* approach – going from one fundraising campaign to another with no long-term view ☐ Lack of understanding of role of fundraising by other departments ☐ Inability to say NO to some fundraising proposals	☐ Increased competition from other not for profits ☐ Vulnerability due to downturn in economy ☐ Increase in number of copy cat fundraising products – diluting your effectiveness ☐ Adverse government policies ☐ New competitors like National Lottery ☐ Changing donor behaviour ☐ Adverse demographic changes

Figure 3.2 SWOT analysis: fundraising

Portfolio analysis

Every department or organisation has a range of products and services. Some appear to be doing very well and are happily seen as cash cows, but others are making little money. Portfolio analysis lets you take an overview of your portfolio, identify its strong and weak components and decide which you should keep in the future.

This useful technique, often called a 'business portfolio matrix', is a two-dimensional graph made up of two variables. Plotting two variables of key importance to your organisation or department can reveal an interesting picture of what projects are worth keeping, known as the 'stars', and those which would be better dropped, the 'dead dogs'. The in-betweens, the 'cash cows' and the 'problem children', also emerge.

For fundraising a key set of variables is the amount of money raised, versus the amount of personnel effort, both staff and volunteer, put into it. No one wants to continue running events which literally wear people out while yielding relatively little. Figure 3.3 shows a number of projects in each category.

Question marks and problem children

Fundraising projects falling in the upper-right quadrant of the matrix have been named question marks or problem children. These ventures require a lot of effort and so they are often quite close to the heart. However, they yield little in cash terms. The manager has to decide if putting more effort in will increase the yield or if the venture be replaced. Hence the 'question mark'.

Stars

Projects with high yields and high involvement rank as stars. They make a lot of money, enthuse people and radiate the feel good factor associated with success.

New stars have to be monitored to make sure they don't turn into a problem child after a number of years, with continuing high involvement but a declining yield.

Cash cows

Fundraising projects which generate a lot of cash with little effort are cash cows. They continue to yield money over and above the amount of effort needed to run them. Many of today's cash cows were yesterday's stars. They may not be capable of future growth, but they are a very valuable part of any fundraising portfolio. They can be milked for reliable cash, which can underwrite the new stars of tomorrow. Again, they must be watched to ensure they don't turn into dead dogs.

Dead dogs

Fundraising projects with low effort and low yield are dead dogs. They have a low growth potential and are usually at the end of their product cycle.

	Fundraising Yield HIGH	Fundraising Yield LOW
H **I** **G** **H** **E** **F** **F** **O** **R** **T**	**STARS** **High Yield** **High Effort**	**PROBLEM** **CHILDREN** **Low Yield** **High Effort**
L **O** **W** **E** **F** **F** **O** **R** **T**	**CASH COWS** **High Yield** **Low Effort**	**DEAD DOGS** **Low Yield** **Low Effort**

Figure 3.3 Portfolio analysis

They are unlikely to turn into cash cows or stars. They are usually ready for replacement.

Implications for fundraising planning

The principal use of this approach is to draw attention to where you are placing your resources and to what effect. You identify the characteristics of your fundraising projects and where they fit into the matrix. You can then reassess them and decide their future role in your planned programme.

Step 3: Assess whether you are achieving the maximum

After establishing which are your most successful activities and the ones you intend to develop to new heights, it is useful to apply two further concepts to these projects to ensure your success. They are the product cycle and the Pareto principle.

The product cycle

Each fundraising or PR product has a life cycle or product cycle. It's useful to see where your major campaigns and fundraising ventures fit into the product cycle. It can help you predict the future mix of your planned programme.

Analysing particular programmes and campaigns

This is an idea taken from marketing practitioners. Products and services are seen to go through a cycle from their first use right through until they are no longer selling. When marketing a product this cycle is taken into account.

In recent years fundraisers and PR people have begun to notice this cycle appearing in their activities. It would be foolish for any fundraiser to assume a never-ending supply of money from any one source. Large motif campaigns and annual PR campaigns are particularly prone to this as they start slowly, build steadily, then decline after a couple of peak years. Figure 3.4 explains this.

When you are examining your fundraising or PR operations, check each of your main activities against a product cycle chart. It can be very informative. Imagine the difference between a fundraising department with all its products in the decline phase and one which has new products coming on line just as the 'old favourites' are ending. Where would you rather be?

Four stages of the product cycle

In monitoring any fundraising or PR initiatives you will observe four stages:

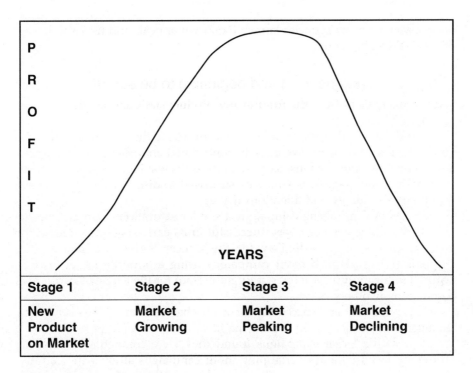

Figure 3.4 Product lifecycle

Stage 1: New product on the market

In fundraising you often have to create a demand for your product. In launching a special appeal for a major disability charity, organisers have to create a demand for the product. They have to assume that people *want* to contribute.

If you launch an unusual campaign like a huge sleep-in or a nationwide coffee morning you are launching a new product. Many not for profits don't like the risk associated with being first and possibly failing. They often prefer to see another organisation risk this stage and survive. They may then adapt and improve on this original idea and move on to the next stage.

Stage 2: Market growing

At this stage your product or service is in the marketplace and growing. With a national motif campaign this would take place in year 2 when you are over the teething problems and your motif is selling in greater numbers.

Third world charities often observe this stage when they launch a special appeal for a disaster in a third world country. They launch an appeal and simultaneously the media picks up alarming reports from that country. Media interest becomes intense and the general public is bombarded with news. Many similar agencies launch their own appeals and new specialised agencies may be set up.

Stage 3: Market peaking and beginning to be saturated

At this stage yield from the fundraising product stalls and levels off before eventually declining.

With third world agencies, it becomes obvious to the late arrivals that the most interested donors have already contributed and now they are appealing to the less interested just as media interest is waning. These late arrivals – usually smaller agencies – may be surprised to discover that interest can drop quite suddenly and donations dry up.

With other fundraising campaigns a similar saturation can occur, particularly if an idea has been very successful in its early stages. In Ireland the heady success of Daffodil Day for the Cancer Society led many other organisations to launch motif campaigns using a butterfly for arthritis, a carnation for multiple sclerosis, a forget-me-not for the Kidney Association, among many others.

They were all very successful for a number of years. However, many smaller organisations then copied the idea, often at the local level, until a number of the larger campaigns found they were competing with many different, localised and overlapping motif campaigns all over the country. Truly, they were the killing of the goose that laid the golden egg.

Stage 4: Market declining

At this stage many voluntary organisations are forced to abandon this type of fundraising activity and move on to something new. The emergence of a variation of the theme day is a case in point – this is, coffee mornings, tea days, 'wear jeans to work' days. Before long 'coffee mornings' and 'tea afternoons' are commonplace and the cycle starts all over again.

With third world organisations you see the emergence of themed appeals replacing appeals for particular countries. This comes from the realisation that you can only interest donors in the plight of a country for so long before they ask why the problem hasn't been solved. With the decline of interest in a particular country you see the emergence of a campaign on an issue – lack of access to water or women's needs, for example – emerging as the new 'marketing product'.

Driving forces in fundraising

One drawback to product cycle analysis is the difficulty in predicting how long each stage will last. So to complement this approach it is often useful to look at the driving forces in Table 3.3 which may be having an impact on the fundraising process.

Table 3.3 Six driving forces in fundraising

1. Changes in donors and how they give
Shifts in donor behaviour along with the emergence of new donors can force a change in how your fundraising is carried out. This is a key area and more is written in chapter 5.

2. Product innovations
New fundraising products can broaden the donor base and rejuvinate your donor. They strengthen the organisation's appeal, usually at the expense of other not for profits which are sticking to old products such as flag days.

3. Process innovation
Frequent and important changes in technology and communications all impact on fundraising. Direct mail is a fast-growing cornerstone of many fundraising departments – it is getting more and more focused as new software is making analysis more sophisticated and accessible.

4. Marketing and PR innovations
When not for profits initiate novel or clever ways to attract attention to their cause, they can create a wave of interest, widen media attention and increase donations. Consider the late Princess Diana's involvement with the British Red Cross to highlight the issue of land mines in Angola.

5. Entry of other not for profits
Every day sees a new fundraising campaign. Not only can the number of not for profits affect you but also the number of fundraisers adopting similar products and approaches to you. Overcrowding in the market and saturation of an area with one approach can be damaging.

6. Changes in cost efficiency
Fundraisers are extremely conscious of controlling or even eliminating costs. However, there are always opportunities to reduce costs and the net returns on fundraising campaigns such as direct mail are very sensitive to cost control.

The Pareto principle

This principle states that 80 per cent of your productivity will come from 20 per cent of your effort. In fundraising and PR terms, it's wise not to confuse activity with accomplishment. It has enormous implications for a review of fundraising or PR programmes.

You can make a quick list of all your fundraising projects or PR campaigns. Apply the Pareto principle to them. You'll find some fundraising activities such as major donor campaigns can yield a large donation, while flag days take up a huge amount of time for a much lower yield. While you may continue to work on some high energy / low yield projects you can consciously seek out and increase the number of high yield / low energy ones.

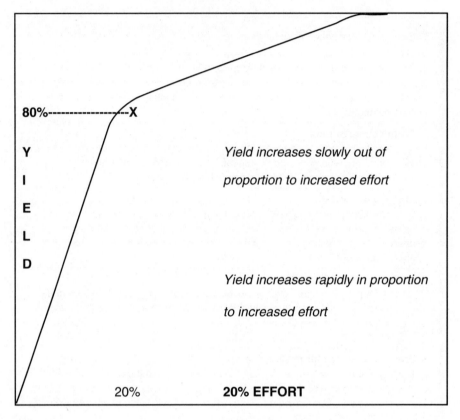

Figure 3.5 Pareto point optimum yield for least effort

Your analysis of the present situation will indicate which activities are yielding the most income. You will find that the Pareto principle applies here. You must plan to concentrate on the 20 per cent of your fundraising activities with the 80 per cent yield.

The fourth and final step

When you have completed your analysis you will be ready to set your goals against a realistic assessment of the current situation. The next chapter deals with the crucial process of setting goals for success. You will know which activities to phase out and which will reward you for time and effort spent on them. However, neither fundraising nor public relations exists in isolation, so before proceeding to set your goals you must also look at the recent strategic performance of the organisation as a whole. Here are some indicators worth looking at:

☐ Is the organisation's market share rising or falling?

☐ Is the organisation making a profit or not?

☐ If it is returning a surplus, how does the profile look over the past five years? Is it climbing or fluctuating at random?

☐ How is the organisation doing relative to others in the same sector?

Summary points

1. Before attempting any planning process you must review the existing situation.
2. For fundraisers, getting a financial overview is crucial. Survey existing income.
3. To get an historical view of fundraising look back over the past five years.
4. A SWOT analysis will let you see the strengths, weaknesses, opportunities and threats.
5. A portfolio analysis will identify prospects worth keeping and those which should be dropped.
6. The 7S Framework will help you plan your strategy knowing your seven variables.
7. The product cycle helps you decide where your prospects are on the growth, peak and decline cycle.
8. The Pareto principle helps you identify if you are working on the prospects which will give you the most return on effort.
9. Don't forget to take a look at the overall performance of the organisation.

4

SETTING GOALS FOR SUCCESS

Introduction

It is vital to set medium and long-term goals for any voluntary organisation's fundraising and PR activities. This chapter explains the concept of
goal-setting with particular reference to fundraising and public relations. A
set of practical tools is provided to equip you to write a set of medium and
long-term goals for your organisation. Easy-to-use charts enable you to start
setting SMART goals and to allocate the necessary time to achieve them.

Setting goals

*Doing too many things isn't always a good idea – no matter how much better
you think you can do them than someone else.*

– Dan Cianipi

Goals are needed for every result that is considered very important to
success.

For a not for profit organisation goals are set for key result areas. These
include:

☐ Annual growth in income
☐ Number of members each year
☐ Reputation for service
☐ Ability to survive fluctuations in income, new services

A not for profit might set the following goals:

☐ 15 per cent growth in income per annum
☐ 1,000 new members each year
☐ Build reputation for services to their client group
☐ Medium-range plan to ensure financial stability in period of reduced
fundraising or drop off in income from wills
☐ One new service to be launched each year, backed up by one or two to be
researched and developed each year.

Individual departments – e.g. fundraising or public relations – while being aware of the overall picture, must set their own goals.

Why fundraising goals are important

Fundraising by its nature is a speculative business. It is easy to say that we can't predict income from a fundraising campaign. It is even possible to get away with that level of vagueness for a while. However, most fundraisers know that the bottom line appears very quickly, especially as many more fundraisers work to agreed income targets.

To achieve an annual target, it is vital to set smaller, achievable goals. These should be staged evenly across the year, as far as possible, to spread the workload. This level of spread also allows for some disappointments and failures. After one disappointing venture it is good to know that another is on its way which could balance out the figures.

Long- and short-term goals

Both long- and short-term goals are needed. Long-term goals have two functions. First, they raise the issue of what actions you have to take now to be able to reach the targeted long-range goal. Second, fundraisers have to consider today's decisions and actions in the light of the long-range goal. This long-term view will stop you basing your decisions on what is expedient in the immediate future.

Short-range goals clearly state the immediate results to be achieved. They tell you the speed at which your fundraising needs to move as well as the level of performance needed. They are your commitment to produce known results in a specific period. In other words how much money, and by when.

Your short- and long-range goals can be the same. For example, if you want to raise overall income by 15 per cent per annum – a long-range goal – you can target a 15 per cent increase on each project in the short term. Or they can differ. If, for example, you are starting to build a fundraising department from scratch and your predicted annual income from direct mail in five years is £1 million per annum, your short-term goal could be to plan to increase income gradually until you reach that level in year 5.

Performance goals

Unless your department's aims and plans are turned into *measurable* performance targets and there is real commitment to achieving them, there is a real risk that the department's aims will end up as a nice document sitting on a shelf. Experience shows that results-oriented goal-setting is crucial to raising funds.

Spelling out targets in a specific, measurable way and then holding

Table 4.1 Common objections to setting targets in not for profits

The Objection	The Answer
☐ We're a not for profit organisation. We don't set targets, we respond to need.	☐ Planning allows the best use of resources to meet needs. In reality no not for profit can help everyone who asks it.
☐ We can't set targets, we have to be able to help everyone.	☐ Planning allows you to get the maximum use of meagre resources and increase the numbers helped.
☐ We don't have time to set targets.	☐ If we don't make time for setting targets we'll always be involved in putting out fires.
☐ Only commercial companies set targets – it is not for not for profits.	☐ Not true. With decreasing resources and increasing demands on not for profits more and more time is being spent on strategic and operating targets.
☐ What do we do if we have an emergency and have to respond?	☐ Plans are not set in stone. We can always respond to an emergency, but when it's over we won't wander around lost – we'll go back and take up our plan.
☐ The committee likes freedom to do what interests them.	☐ Committee members give their time freely but it is still a precious commodity. They won't object to effective use of their time – especially when they see results.

yourself, other staff and volunteer committees accountable for reaching them has two outcomes. First, people become more purposeful and strategic in what they do. Second, it provides you with a benchmark for judging how good the fundraising performance has been.

Performance goals should be *quantifiable* and *measurable* and should have a completion date.

Set achievable goals

You should never set goals at a level which you or someone else feels would be good to achieve. Wishful thinking has no real part in goal-making. Staff

Table 4.2 The 'SMART' approach: five key points for setting goals

Specific:	A goal should relate to a single, specific logic.
Measurable:	A goal should be measurable, in quantitative terms.
Achievable:	A goal should be challenging, but achievable.
Result:	A goal should relate to a result not its performance.
Timed:	A goal should contain a time deadline for completion.

in not for profit organisations have many taskmasters, including their boss, one or many volunteer committees, the overall council and, of course, people they serve. These groups may have many different hopes and aspirations. Setting realistic goals in those circumstances can be difficult.

Certainly, challenging goals should be set to stretch the organisation or department, but not so challenging that they defeat the staff. Goals must be achievable.

You need to be aware of the capacity of your department and what it can achieve when pushed. This will affect the limit achievable without change of some kind in terms of resources.

A quick guide to setting goals is set out in Table 4.2.

Look around you before you set goals

Goals cannot be set in isolation of the players in the sector in which you are operating. To ensure your goals are achievable you need to take account of a number of factors:

☐ What level of performance is possible in the present economic climate? Your level of performance will be influenced by how much disposable income people have.
☐ How are other not for profits in your sector? How many are there? You may think your cause is unique, but people are influenced by how many times they have been asked for money by similar not for profits. Blurring of identity between two similar organisations may work to the detriment of both.

The key point to remember is that the overall goal must be supported by a clearly defined set of performance targets for each member of staff and each active committee member. This leads to a clear view of what is expected and who is responsible for achieving it. Done well, this approach energises

Table 4.3 How goal-setting should reach all levels

£850,000 needed to fund costs of one year

Director and Board set goal

Fundraiser and Fundraising Committee reach goals

Grants Foundation and Trusts	Major Donor	Direct Mail	Special Events	National Campaign
1 staff member to raise £50,000 net	Fundraiser & Director & 3 Board members to raise £150,000	2 staff to raise £250,000 net	1 staff & 3 special committees to run 3 events. Goal to raise £300,000	1 staff member to run 1 national campaign to raise £100,000
Goal is to approach 6 organisations to raise £50,000	Goal is to have each Board member raise £50,000	Goal is to have 6 separate mailing campaigns	3 Fundraising Committee members to chair a separate committee for each event. Goal is £100,000 net each event	Goal to raise £100,000 net
Pay attention to deadlines for applications	This could take a year to complete	Mailings to be phased over the year	An event in May, September and December	6 months lead-in time. Start in January and run Campaign in June

everyone involved, creates a results-oriented approach and unites all involved in fundraising.

Generating ideas and goals

When setting your goals it is important to be open to new ideas and influences. It's difficult to generate new programmes and events on demand. However, there are a number of ways to produce new ideas.

At least once a year have a brainstorming session with people in the media, artists, entertainers, writers, film people, actors, teachers and lots of young people. You'll find lots of ideas will emerge. Make a note of them all, even the most outrageous and impractical ones. Store them for later. You'll find that one or two gems will emerge which will form the basis of a fundraiser or PR campaign for next year.

An alternative is to hold a competition for students. Approach a local college of art and design, media studies or marketing and ask the Director for help. These young people are the trendsetters and marketers of the future.

Set up a committee of young people who'll meet twice a year and involve them in your work. Listen to them. Note their comments and act on them.

Key success factors

Key success factors determine financial and competitive success in any endeavour. They are crucial to fundraising and public relations. They change from year to year as circumstances change and need to be constantly reviewed. For any given planning period they should be clearly identified and set out. They help you decide which things are most important in order to achieve your goals.

Table 4.4 Possible key success factors

Fundraising	Public Relations
☐ Cost efficiencies	☐ Good programmes and services to talk about
☐ Visibility in community	
☐ Skilled, well-motivated staff	☐ Totally untarnished reputation of not for profit
☐ Totally untarnished reputation	
☐ Large body of well-motivated volunteers	☐ Continuous flow of creative ideas
	☐ Keeping up to date media contact lists
☐ Well-organised branch structure around country.	
	☐ A reputation for reliability and honesty in dealing with media
☐ Clear identification of benefits to donor for their donation	
	☐ Cultivation of contacts in relevant sections of media
☐ Acute awareness of what competitors are doing	
☐ Services and products which are of relevance to target groups	
☐ Clear identification of what donations are spent on	
☐ Administration costs in relation to income	
☐ Regular production of innovative products.	

Table 4.5 Setting goals the SMART way

Specific Goals	Quantify Goal	Is it Achievable?	Result Expected	Time Deadline
1 GOAL				
2 GOAL				
3 GOAL				
4 GOAL				
5 GOAL				
6 GOAL				
7 GOAL				
8 GOAL				
9 GOAL				
10 GOAL				

Table 4.6 Allocate time to achieve your annual goals

Goals	Jan/ Feb	Mar/ Apr	May/ June	Jul/ Aug	Sep/ Oct	Nov/ Dec
1						
2						
3						
4						
5						
6						
7						
8						
9						
10						

Summary points

1. Setting goals is vital to ensure you are focused on getting results.
2. The SMART way to set goals ensures your goals are specific, measurable, achievable, result-oriented and timed.
3. Goals should be set at all levels in the organisation.
4. Identify your key success factors.
5. Allocate time in the next year to ensure you achieve your goals.

5

PLANNING LONG TERM

Introduction

No planning process is complete unless it includes an evaluation stage. This chapter takes you through a number of checklists which you can use in your evaluations.

Evaluation

One working definition of evaluation I have come across is this: 'The prime purpose of evaluation is to find out if a specific activity has produced the targeted results.' This is a good starting point. Evaluation is a core component of all planning processes. It's the next step after reviewing where you are, deciding where you want to be, setting targets to get there and then evaluating how well you have succeeded.

Annual evaluation

Fundraisers and PR practitioners must carry out an overall evaluation of the year's activities at the end of each financial year. If you have followed the planning processes in this book you will be able to review your annual plan and assess how well – or how badly – you have done.

Programming/Project evaluation

Each fundraising project should be evaluated on completion, starting with a financial evaluation and sometimes involving an assessment of use of volunteers and other parameters.

Evaluation is only as good as the original planning

The quality of any evaluation depends on how much effort went into preparing the original plan. If the plan had quantified and focused targets, then the evaluation has something concrete to work on. If the original aims were vague, like 'We'll run an event to make money for the centre', it is impossible to evaluate how well or how worthwhile the exercise was.

Evaluation depends on clear goals

Fundraising initiatives, particularly when led by voluntary committees, can suffer from a lack of clear goals. This increases with the committee size. Take the example of a special event – a film première – run annually to raise funds. A new chairperson is appointed and decides to question everything and ultimately changes everything. Friends are brought in to help and the staff and committee members don't want to stand in the way of all this new and welcome enthusiasm.

The chairperson decides that the organisation's practice of charging £100 per person is too exclusive and all members of the community should be able to attend. 'We're an inclusive organisation,' goes the cry. Other committee members like this sentiment and so the price drops to £25. It is decided to sell the event to members and in neighbourhood groups.

In the evaluation held after the event the chairperson is thrilled as the event was a sellout and everyone loved it. 'The local community love us – we included them.' But one old hand on the committee points to the budget and comments that income has dropped drastically compared to the previous year while everyone had to work twice as hard as they had to sell to a totally new market. The answer is that it wasn't a fundraiser but a PR exercise for 'giving back to the community'.

The lack of clarity of goals couldn't be starker. What started out as a fundraiser targeted at people willing to pay £100 and with the objective of raising £40,000, turned into a local community PR exercise, made little money, lost the original customers, pleased the community but exhausted the *fundraising* committee and disappointed the fundraiser, who wanted this to fill a gap in the fundraising budget.

If you were asked to evaluate this event, where would you start?

Fundraising evaluation

Evaluation techniques can give you an idea of the 'profitability' of your activities. But first, you need to explore what exactly you want to measure. Table 5.1 will help guide you.

It is always wise to keep track of your donor programmes. Table 5.2 will get you started.

Evaluation has four main purposes for future planning

1. To identify activities which are performing well – to replicate the success and to reward those responsible.

Table 5.1 What fundraisers should evaluate

☐ Income of each event against budget.

☐ Compare income with your budget to see how accurate your budget was.

☐ Real cost in terms of hidden costs.

☐ How much administrative back-up was involved?

☐ Amount of volunteer time to run event.

☐ Certain fundraising ventures are not good as they wear volunteers out with little return.

☐ Length of time to organise event.

☐ It is OK to make a good return but not if it took up all your time.

☐ Ratio of gross income to net income.

☐ It is not worth spending £3 to make £1.

☐ Is this event repeatable?

☐ Special events are only worthwhile if they can be run over a number of years.

☐ Cost of raising each £1.

☐ Number of purchasers of tickets (not number of people attending).

☐ Did I put in place some mechanism for getting the name and address of all the guests?

Table 5.2 Checklist for donor programmes

☐ How many donors do we have?

☐ How often do they give?

☐ How much do they give – average donation?

☐ When did they last give – how many lapsed donors do we have?

☐ How much is it costing to get each new donor?

☐ How much goes on costs of getting or retaining donors?

☐ Do I know how many donors I have in each category, e.g. £10, £20, £100?

☐ Do I know the profile of our organisation's 'average' donor.

2. To identify activities which are not succeeding – to decide how to improve them or to eliminate them.

Table 5.3 Performance indicators

Average gift size

Divide the total amount donated	£200,000	
by number of donations received	1,500	= £133

Average cost per donation

Divide total costs of fundraising	£35,000	
by number of donations	1,500	= £23

Percentage rate of return

Divide the number of responses	1,400	
by numbers of letters sent out	120,000	= 0.01%

Table 5.4 Overall fundraising programme

Performance assessment

Year-end date

Activity	Income last year	Income this year	(Estimated budget)	Cost per £1 raised
	£	£	£	£
Voluntary Income				
Direct mail campaigns				
1.				
2.				
3.				
4.				
Major Gifts				
Workplace Giving				

Covenants

Bequests

Special Events

☐ Large-scale

1.

2.

3.

4.

☐ Small-scale Total

Grants

☐ Government

1.

2.

3.

4.

☐ Foundations/Trusts

5.

6.

7.

8.

Corporate Donations

1.

2.

3.

4.

Sponsorship	
1.	
2.	
TOTALS	

3. To assess the overall plan – were its objectives realistic? – and to revisit the assumptions underlying the plan.
4. To use past experience to guide future planning.

Tracking changing interests

The public's interests and emotions can change rapidly regarding not for profits and charitable giving. Regular evaluation will keep you abreast of these changes and stop major crises arising. Fundraisers and PR staff need to be flexible if they are going to keep pace with donors' shifting interests. Also, you have to be able to put extra effort and resources into campaigns which are going well and transfer resources away from products which are at the end of their product cycle.

Criteria

Percentage participation lets you know what potential donors think of the message you are giving them. If the percentage drops, it is a sign their interest is shifting.

Average donation size

An increasing gift size tells you people like what they see – they are becoming close to you. Average costs per donation are a key element. You must keep a keen eye on this to keep it low and constantly decreasing.

Volunteers

Volunteers are a voluntary organisation's most valuable asset. We discuss the professional ways of recruiting and managing volunteers in chapter 6. However, it is vital to assess what is happening with your volunteers. Knowing you have enough volunteers is vital for future planning of activities. To ensure that you have that supply you must evaluate a number of aspects of your Volunteer Programme.

The key issue is whether your volunteers are staying with the organisation for a reasonable length of time. Table 5.5 will help you get an overview.

Table 5.5 Volunteer assessment

☐ Number of volunteers this year/last year.

☐ Number of volunteers associated with each activity.

☐ Average length of stay of volunteers.

☐ Activities volunteers like. Do we know why?

☐ Do we have an age profile of our volunteers?

☐ Do we have a volunteer recruitment programme?

☐ What are the elements of it?

☐ How many volunteers did we get from each element?

☐ Are we listening to our volunteers?

☐ How? – Surveys
      – Face to face
      – Focus groups

☐ Do we have elements of a volunteer recognition programme in place?

1.

2.

3.

☐ Is someone on the staff responsible for volunteers?

Summary points

1. You must evaluate all your activities to see if they have produced the targeted results.
2. Evaluation can only work if clear targets and goals have been set.
3. As well as evaluating the overall programme you should also evaluate each fundraising and PR activity.
4. Evaluate your donors constantly so that you can improve your performance.
5. Evaluate your volunteers' work, commitment, turnover.

6

UNDERSTANDING YOUR DONORS AND SAYING THANK YOU

Introduction

This chapter focuses on the most important component of fundraising: the donor. It discusses the reasons why people give money, advises on analysing your donors and discusses two relatively untapped sources of donors – young people and women.

The two most important words in a fundraiser's vocabulary are 'thank you'. Giving donors recognition is too important to be left to chance, so procedures must be put in place to ensure all donors are treated appropriately.

Why people give

There are many reasons why people give to not for profits, the principal one being that they have been asked. It may seem obvious, but it is none the less true, that many donations, particularly large ones, come about because the right person asked, at the right time, for the right amount. If you don't ask, you won't receive.

Various studies over the years by not for profit organisations have produced lists of reasons why people donate. From a review of a number of lists the following emerge as the major reasons:

- ☐ Guilt
- ☐ Fear
- ☐ To make a difference to society
- ☐ Belief in your cause
- ☐ To repay for services you gave or continue to give them
- ☐ Someone close to them persuaded them
- ☐ Ego
- ☐ To receive public recognition
- ☐ To feel good

☐ To contribute to their local community
☐ Good business reasons, good PR pays back
☐ Like to attend special events
☐ They have made a lot of money and want to give something back

The most important thing to remember about your research is how you can use the findings to improve your returns. You do not need to be judgemental. The most effective way to find what motivates people is to ask them and listen to their answers. Listening requires that you pay attention and give positive feedback. Every fundraiser should spend time developing good listening skills. If necessary, take a course. It will be money well spent.

If your fundraising is accompanied by a clear, concise statement of what you do and the benefits to the community, you will generate more interest in your organisation.

Analysing your donors

The importance of analysing and understanding your donors can't be overemphasised.

Without an analysis of your donors – done continuously – a not for profit cannot discover which fundraising strategies work, what interests donors and volunteers most and which PR activities were most effective.

Analysis allows you to know your donors extremely well and enhances your communication with them.

Objections to donor research

Many not for profits say they can't afford research. It is too disruptive and anyway, they are too busy sending out letters or organising special events to spend time finding out about their donors. This reluctance is found most commonly in medium to small voluntary organisations which are hard-pressed for resources.

The reality is that each organisation has its own way of working, different needs and sends out different messages. Each package is unique. You can't just take a fundraising tool off the shelf, use it without understanding whom you are approaching and hope to make lots of money. Yet, fundraising without donor research is just that.

Adaptation to donors

The ability to be flexible and responsive to donors' needs and their expectations of your organisation is a key element of success in fundraising.

Table 6.1 Preliminary information about donors

Demographics

☐ Gender
☐ Age
☐ Income
☐ Education
☐ Family size

Geography

Relating a particular population to its geographical
location, e.g., urban/rural/suburban.

The more you listen to donors and adapt to their concerns, the more they appreciate it and the more they respond to your appeals.

Collect objective information

Gather information about your donors *per se*. Do not collect data to justify a particular campaign or approach. You will only persuade donors to give if you know their needs and respond to them. Next, move on to answer the needs of different groups.

Tools of analysis

Segmentation

This process allows you to move on from knowing your donors' needs to dividing your target market into different segments. Segmentation allows you to identify the most relevant groups or target markets and match them with a tailored approach.

Consider the following:

☐ How recently did the person make a donation – is it time to ask again?
☐ How much did they give – are they 'small' or 'major' donors?
☐ How often do they give – are they regular or one-off donors?

These questions are important to your long-term fundraising success. Knowing when to ask for a repeat or second donation is crucial. Treating small and major donors differently is essential. Major donors deserve a more significant form of recognition. Regular donors are showing their loyalty to you and need special thanks or they could feel taken for granted.

Checklist for donor analysis

☐ Can I segment my donors by their level of giving, or their frequency of giving?
☐ Do I know why they are giving to our organisation?
☐ Do I know what motivates them to give?
☐ Do I know which of our programmes they like best?
☐ Do I check regularly to see what they think of what we do with their money?

How do I find out what donors think?

The simple answer is: ask them. The way you ask and how many you approach depends on cost and your budget. Techniques include questionnaires, phoning, face-to-face interviews and focus groups. Focus groups are when you bring a group of your donors together and use a facilitator to discover what they feel about an issue.

You will find an approach that suits your resources. The crucial point is that you ask your donors their opinions – even if it is only a small sample, it gives you valuable feedback.

Recent research trends

Some interesting indicators of people's giving trends are pointed out by James Banks and Sarah Tanner in the 1997 edition of *Dimensions of the Voluntary Sector*. They used data from the Family Expenditure Survey over the years 1984 to 1993/94, which included more than 70,000 households. The results shown in Table 6.2.

Untapped donors 1: young people

Charitable giving among young people is declining. Recent research commissioned by Charities Aid Foundation has shown that young people in the 18–22 age group were giving less to charity in 1994 than in 1974.

We seem to be making it difficult for young people to give.

☐ Direct mail campaigns do not target them, focusing instead on middle-class, older people.
☐ Fundraisers are channelling people into giving by regular planned donations, covenants, payroll deduction or using credit cards. Young people generally don't use these means.
☐ Young people watch TV and videos and go to pubs and nightclubs, so why not make more use of these channels?

Table 6.2 Long-term trends in giving

☐ A 10 per cent increase in income increases the probability of giving by 1 percentage point. The size of donations also increases – but by more than 10 per cent, i.e., charitable giving is a 'luxury good'.

☐ Older people are more likely to give and also likely to give more, conditional on their level of income. The effect of increasing the age of the head of the household by ten years is to raise the probability of giving by 4 percentage points.

☐ Education and occupation have positive effects on giving over and above income.

☐ Children and the proportion of females in the household also increase both participation and the level of giving. A simple comparison of households with and without children would suggest that the presence of children reduces the probability of giving but, controlling for income and age, children have a positive effect.

☐ Except for a small number of major campaigns, little use is made of television. Almost no use is made of videos and apart from some local initiatives the places young people frequent have not been targeted in any concerted way.

☐ Young people use the internet and slowly use of this as a fundraising tool is increasing.

You should find ways to target this sector, as they are a new group. However, innovative methods are needed. One approach could be via payroll deduction as young people in employment respond to salary deduction schemes.

Certain types of causes appeal to young people – AIDS, homelessness, the third world and certain environmental causes. Young people can identify with these causes and will become involved.

Untapped donors 2: women

Traditionally, fundraisers sought out middle-aged, middle-class men because they 'controlled' the household and, by sheer numbers, the country's 'wealth'. Now as fundraisers find the number of voluntary donors dropping this view must be challenged.

Women represent a new and growing source of donations, and fundraising potential among women is surprisingly large. Yet few voluntary organisations are focusing on this sector. By learning how to understand women's giving patterns and by setting up special programmes to involve women donors you can tap this growing source.

Joseph Rowntree Foundation research, published in March 1996, showed one in five women are now the household's higher earner – a threefold rise in the past decade.

Women have become a major earning force. The typical married or cohabiting woman who works full-time brings home more than 40 per cent of the family income.

Since 1964 the number of female employees in the UK has increased from 8.1 million to 10.9 million, while male employees have decreased from 14.7 million to 11.1 million This rise in the number of female earners is expected to continue. Changes in employment patterns with more women available for work and the shift from manufacturing to services will add to this.

Research has examined the effect of household income and age on giving to charity. More analysis of female-led households or households with equal income between men and women could help organisations wishing to target this group.

Table 6.3 Reaching women donors

☐ Tailor your message to women, take a lesson from the advertising world. Do not rehash the techniques that worked with male donors. Develop special messages.

☐ Understand what the women donors want, e.g. women donors like to be involved in discussion regarding programmes seeking their support.

☐ Avoid 'peer pressure' messages in your literature – women are less status-conscious than men.

☐ Women like to get the overview as well as pertinent details. They are more into specifics than men – if you do not supply them, they won't respond.

☐ Women like their money to make a difference so they give to specific causes they know and understand. Achieving that requires work by the fundraiser. General appeals to their good nature from good causes won't work.

☐ Look to your women volunteers. Many women stay at the basic volunteer level long after the organisations should have invited them onto their Councils or Boards or cultivated them into major donors.

☐ Many women will support programmes which will directly benefit and advance other women. Check your organisation's plans and see if there are programmes specially targeted at women.

☐ Women care more about building a relationship with the organisation than just getting recognition. So spend time building up your organisation's relationship with a potential woman donor.

As a fundraiser you should look at your database to find out the giving habits of your women donors.

Donor recognition: saying thank you

The two most important words in a fundraiser's vocabulary are 'thank you'. Saying thank you is so simple, but so easily overlooked. When planning any fundraising project always include the 'thank you' stage, preferably before the evaluation stage.

Effective fundraisers depend on repeat business. They want people to give on an annual basis, people to come to events each year and people to collect on annual flag days. It is too difficult to start each year from scratch, so it is vital to have carry-over fundraising projects. To achieve this you must keep your donors and volunteers faithful to the organisation. The single most effective way of doing this is to show them that you care and appreciate them.

Relations with donors, like friendships, require time and effort to keep up the contact, show interest in one another, share ideas and goals and to work together. Formal donor recognition programmes are one way of ensuring this happens. If donors are included in evaluations, policy think-in days and training sessions, they become more than mere sources of money.

Putting the donor first

'Putting the donor first' is the guiding principle of any successful fundraiser. It requires knowing how to match their needs and wishes with your organisation's aims. Getting to know your donor requires work and time. Once you have expended all that effort to get regular donations or a major gift, do you want to risk losing the donor because you failed to thank them?

It takes more time to get new donors than to retain the ones you already have. Businesses know this and concentrate on customer loyalty programmes.

It makes good financial sense to thank your donors. Make giving to your organisation a pleasant experience by handling the donation and giving thanks in a professional way.

Have you really said 'thank you'?

A lot has been written about thanking donors and acknowledging their contributions. The most important aspect is the thank you itself, the recognition follows automatically. To ensure that the all-important thank you is given it is useful to put a formal procedure in place.

Procedures for saying 'thank you'

Immediate thank you

A letter of thanks should be sent, ideally within 24 hours (but never later than 48 hours) of receiving a donation. Ensure you have the staff or volunteer resources available to make this rule workable.

Levels of thanks matches the size of donation

Sizeable donations should be acknowledged by the Director or Chief Executive. Major donations should be acknowledged by the President or equivalent.

A personal thanks

Decide on a level of donation over which the person will be thanked in person by phone. This will vary with the size of the organisation. A donation of £5,000 to a small community organisation in its first year is a major gift but not so to a large multi-million pound charity.

Be innovative in your thanks

Give a token of your thanks that is appropriate to your organisation. During the Arthritis Foundation's Butterfly week we sent major donors a butterfly of some sort – anything that depicted butterflies: jewellery, crystal, books, art. They were greatly prized. A theatre company or dance company could send a programme or ballet shoes autographed by one of their stars.

Be personal in your thanks

If you know your donor's interests (you are likely to know a lot if it is a major donor), give them a special thank you gift. For example, if the person is fond of books get a first edition or an autographed copy of one of their favourite author's books.

Involve board members

Make sure your President and board members know about major gifts. It will mean a lot to your donor if he/she is informally thanked by one of their peers. The worst situation would be if the President was unaware of the gift and failed to mention it to the donor at a social gathering.

Going beyond thank you to customer satisfaction

How can you improve the customer service elements of your fundraising? The following are a number of pointers:

Make contributing easy

Offer a number of ways to contribute and allow the donor to use the one most convenient to them – not you. Accept cheques, credit cards, post office orders – whatever.

Process financial transactions promptly

Clear credit card pledges, etc., on a daily basis.

Deal with correspondence

In addition to the thank you letter, deal with correspondence efficiently. If donors ask questions, answer them. If donors want information materials, send them out promptly.

Keep accurate records

Get people's names and addresses right.

Encourage complaints

Encourage complaints and handle them well. If donors care enough to complain, they care enough to keep giving. Finally, act on the complaints – after all it is free advice.

Improving your donor recognition

It is important not to get complacent about thanking donors. It is tempting to think that once your procedures are in place you can move on to

---

Table 6.4 Checklist for donor recognition

☐ Ensure the organisation has a firm and visible commitment to its donors.

☐ Learn about your donors' interests – so you can meet them.

☐ Educate staff and volunteers to know their role in donor recognition.

☐ Have a code in your organisation for treating all donors with great respect.

☐ Ensure board members are personally involved in cultivating donors.

☐ Set out clear written procedures for thanking donors.

☐ Set out clear steps for dealing with major gifts.

☐ Measure and continuously improve donor recognition procedures of the organisation.

something else. Not so. You should build in evaluation steps. Use focus groups, surveys and meet people on a one-to-one basis. Keep asking how you can improve your processes.

Make it a practice to question everything – and do it from the donor's perspective. Review the whole process of your donor's interaction with the organisation. Don't view any one part in isolation. Donors are very volatile and can change quickly. As a fundraiser you must know how they are being treated.

Regularly review how the systems in the fundraising office affect donors. Develop your office procedures and your personnel to ensure an excellent donor experience.

Focus groups

Focus groups are considered qualitative research because they give you an insight into the deeper feelings of your donors. They usually involve 8–12 donors meeting for approximately two hours with a facilitator to discuss their views on some element of the organisation. They are useful if you want to get views on any aspect of the organisation.

Examples include:

- [ ] The draft plans for a new fundraising campaign.
- [ ] An existing fundraising campaign.
- [ ] An awareness or PR campaign.
- [ ] Your donor recognition procedures.
- [ ] Your newsletter.

The special thanks: thanking major donors

It takes a lot of thought and planning to come up with the appropriate recognition for a major donor.

You must know about the person to make sure that your thanks are appropriate and memorable. If you don't know anything about the person, ask. Go to the library and read up about them and their business or foundation, or ask board members.

You must work out your means of recognition on a case-by-case basis. Some donors may want no publicity, so you will have to thank them privately and in person – your board might hold a private lunch or meeting.

If the donor is happy with or actively seeks public recognition, then you can design something particular to that individual.

If your major donor is a company, then you should consult the PR or Marketing Department. You could also encourage them to send their employees to visit your organisation to see how you operate.

Sometimes it is very difficult to find the appropriate way of saying thank you. This can arise when a donor has been making donations for a number of years – increasing the donation a little each time. This requires imagination. One very unusual gesture I've seen is giving that kind of person an 'Honorary Doctorate in Philanthropy'. It gets lots of publicity and it points to the long-term nature of the contributions.

The personal touch

The most effective way of thanking someone who has given a sizeable donation is to pick up the phone and thank them personally. Do it on the day you receive the donation. You must also send the usual written forms of thanks, but the immediate and personal gesture of thanks cannot be bettered.

Table 6.5 The ultimate service: small touches

☐ Send a thank you card every year-end.

☐ Bring special presents when visiting special donors.

☐ After meeting a special donor, send a follow-up note.

☐ Remember facts and figures – make notes of birthdays, anniversaries, children's names, recent donations.

☐ Make it easy for potential donors,

Summary points

1. Knowing why donors give is a fundamental start to fundraising.
2. Every fundraiser needs to analyse their donors systematically.
3. Segmentation is a useful starting point for donor analysis.
4. Find ways to appeal to young donors.
5. Target women for donations and customise your appeals to women.
6. Saying thank you is fundamental to successful fundraising.
7. Remember: always put the donor first.
8. Go beyond thank you to customer satisfaction.
9. Improve your donor recognition by listening – use focus groups.
10. You need to give major donors special recognition.

YOUR EIGHT STEPS TO A SUCCESSFUL VOLUNTEER PROGRAMME

Introduction

Constant focus on short-term fundraising distorts your whole approach. It influences how you structure your fundraising department, manage your volunteers and staff, set targets and plan your associated public relations – in short, everything is affected by short termism.

One thing that strikes people examining the fundraising world is the turnover of voluntary personnel, especially in the younger age groups. People tend to start enthusiastically, work hard, use up all their contacts and eventually burn out. Fundraising volunteers can be like shooting stars – brilliant for a while but doomed. It is important to avoid that shooting star effect and to ensure that your fundraising programme includes aspects that build for the future.

For any staff member in a voluntary organisation, their most valuable support is enthusiastic and well-motivated volunteers. In fact, the National Council For Voluntary Organisations (NCVO) estimates that 1.1 million people work as trustees in the voluntary sector. However, in most voluntary organisations we wait until we have a crisis before we stop to think about our volunteers. This is especially true of committee and council members. Failure to devote time and effort to developing volunteers and committee members can come back to haunt you. Unfortunately, it is often in times of crises that the problems surface.

Not for profits are all about people and volunteers, yet investment in developing people is generally not seen as a priority. Don't make this mistake. Make your volunteers, your voluntary committees and your staff a top priority. Learn to understand them, their motivations and, above all, recognise their efforts. If you follow the eight steps outlined in this chapter you will greatly improve your volunteer programme.

The eight steps to a successful volunteer programme

Over the past fifteen years I have worked with volunteers in a large number of organisations and I have come up with a series of eight steps which will help you in a very practical way to recruit and keep your volunteers well motivated and so boost your fundraising programme.

Step 1: Take stock of your voluntary committee

The first point to remember about voluntary committees is that they should exist to do a specific job for the organisation, otherwise they are just a talking shop and you can do without them. To ensure effectiveness you need to answer the questions about the fundraising committee set out in Table 7.1.

If you work in a typical not for profit, the answer to many of these questions is probably no. If you want to be more successful at what you do you must immediately address the issue of your volunteer committee.

Step 2: Recruit new members

Start at the beginning. Make an inventory of existing members and identify any gaps in talents, experience and representation, be it gender, race or disability. Have you got representatives of the general membership? Don't

---

Table 7.1 Questions you must ask about the fundraising committee

☐ Have you carefully analysed what talents and experience you would like on your committee?

☐ Have you analysed and listed the talents and experience of the existing committee members?

☐ Have you identified the inevitable gap between the two?

☐ Are you clear about the chairperson's vision for the committee?

☐ Do committee members clearly understand what's expected of them, and do they really understand and identify with the organisation?

☐ Do you have a structured, well thought-out approach to finding new committee members, or do you just gratefully accept someone nominated by an existing member?

☐ Do you have a programme for training and developing committee members?

☐ Are members regularly thanked by the chairperson and by you?

be haphazard in your approach. If you don't think about the categories and gaps, you'll end up with the people put forward by the existing committee.

The key word in recruiting new people is ACTION. Look for people you can count on to show up and to work.

Where to look for new recruits

First look close to home

Look at donors, loyal supporters, members, friends and families of your client groups. They may have given loyal service but have never been asked to serve on a committee. Many people have hidden talents and can develop into real assets.

Look in the business community

Don't look for people at the very top of the career tree. They may be well intentioned but they rarely have time and can become passive committee members, only turning up for the big events, but not doing any consistent or real work.

Look for people who are on their way up and who are willing to work. Look out for rising stars. Read magazines and newspaper profiles, especially in the business sections.

A useful tactic is to ask prominent business people for advice. Assure them you are not targeting them personally, but genuinely looking for advice and suggestions. It works. They may be very willing to give you an hour of their time if there are no strings attached. Such advice is invaluable and cannot be bought.

Don't forget the human dimension. Don't be overwhelmed by the search for particular skills and talents to the exclusion of all else. Always consider the need for fair people, people with good judgement, patient people, good team workers and people with a proven record of working on committees.

Table 7.2 Sources for starting up a committee from scratch

Politicians

Clergy

Local businesses

Chambers of Commerce

Editors or journalists

Before deciding which groups to target consider the following points:

☐ A traditional source of volunteers was *women working within the home*. This is a dwindling resource as more and more women enter the workforce. However, this is balanced by the emergence of the active retired. People are retiring earlier, staying more active and want to be involved, in a positive way, in their community.

☐ *Unemployed people*, be they short- or long-term unemployed, want to be involved in some meaningful activity, as it may give them new skills.

☐ *Full-time employees* are often overlooked as a source of volunteers. Remember the saying 'If you want something done, ask a busy person'. Professional people will be comfortable volunteering time in their area of expertise. You may need a professional PR practitioner to help you with press materials, a copywriter for ads or posters, a printer to advise on printing budgets, a caterer to advise on meals for a special dinner.

☐ *Young people seeking their first job* can be an excellent source of volunteers. A recent PR or marketing graduate may work for a number of months on a big fundraising campaign to get the practical expertise. Colleges may be willing to place students on work experience and you could take advantage of this.

☐ Speaking at *club meetings, senior citizens groups, women's groups, chambers of commerce, Rotary Clubs*, etc. may bring forward volunteers.

☐ Advertising in *national newspapers, local newspapers, business in-house magazines, church newsletters*, etc., can elicit a response. Remember: the more specific your need, the more targeted your approach should be. If you want volunteers from PR or marketing, advertise in their trade or special interest magazines.

☐ Ask your *colleagues*, who are running programmes in the community, to look for fundraising or PR volunteers.

☐ *Former clients of the organisation* make excellent advocates. They often have a genuine and sincere belief in the work of the organisation and can be very effective in persuading people to volunteer.

☐ *One-to-one 'eye balling'* is the best recruitment method there is. When you have located a potential volunteer be specific about your needs, specify the time required and be generous in your charm and appreciation.

☐ *Older people* should not be overlooked as a source of volunteers. The Success of Age Concern, England's Trans Age Action Project, which facilitated 70 volunteers (with no upper age limit) to work with vulnerable children, bears this out. Furthermore, it is worth noting that one in four people in Europe will be over 60 by the year 2020.

☐ *Teenagers* are another group often overlooked. They may not be coming forward as volunteers simply because they are not being asked. Recent research by the American group Independent Sector, based in Washington, found that teenagers are four times more likely to volunteer if they are asked than if left to volunteer themselves.

Table 7.3 Summary of sources of potential volunteers

Women who work at home.

Active, retired people – especially recently retired people.

Unemployed people.

People between jobs or on career breaks.

Professionals in their own area of expertise.

Former clients of the organisation.

Parents and friends of present clients.

New arrivals wanting to get involved in the community.

People with specific hobbies, e.g., art or music.

Don't forget to ask

It may seem obvious, but you only get people to join if you ask them. Putting notices on boards or in newsletters doesn't work. Writing letters puts off the inevitable – you must *talk* to the person.

Be clear about the role of committee members

It is absolutely essential that people who join fundraising committees realise that their role is to *generate funds*. There is nothing more frustrating then someone on the fundraising committee saying, 'I've already raised £40,000 for my son's school to buy new equipment, I'm sorry I can't do anything for you this year.' Far better to be clear what the person's role is before they join the committee rather than having embarrassment later.

Step 3: Enhance performance of committee members

Preparing your new committee members: orientation

Always meet the new committee members before their first committee meeting. Try to get the chairperson to accompany you. Send them all the papers for the next meeting. Prepare a briefing pack – but don't overload them. To start, they will need a brief history of the organisation, an annual report and promotional literature explaining what the organisation does. Then move on to the value and work of their particular committee. Copies of minutes of the last three meetings, a copy of annual plans, a list of other committee members and a brief biography of each member should suffice. Any more and they'll run!

Support your new recruit in the initial stages

Some organisations ask serving committee members to 'adopt' a new member and to keep in touch with them until they find their feet. At the least, they should call the person before the first meeting and they should provide a special welcome at the first meeting. Knowing that someone is expecting you and will introduce you makes an excellent first impression and makes the new recruit feel part of the team.

Keeping committee members motivated

This cannot be overemphasised. After all the trouble that went into finding the right person, initiating them and getting them on board, it is a terrible waste to lose them. The best way to motivate committee members is to acknowledge their efforts.

Recognition – a vital tool in sustaining committees

Recognition and thanks are powerful motivators. The best kind of motivation is ongoing and personal. The chairperson should not only thank individuals at meetings but should telephone the person or drop them a note. Staff members should also write to thank committee members who have been hard working.

Awards, scrolls and plaques are also greatly appreciated as a formal mark of appreciation. They rarely cost much, but mean a great deal. They can be displayed in the person's home or place of business and are often greatly prized.

What do you do about passengers on the committee?

You weed them out. It is often said that you can't sack committee members or volunteers. That isn't true. Realistically, what you want is for them to leave to make way for active, working volunteers. You have to be subtle and sensitive, but you don't have to be inert.

People who do not participate or work should be given the possibility of stepping down. Leaving them in place can quickly demoralise your other committee members.

Volunteer committees – keeping records

It is useful to circulate a chart of attendances at meetings, once a year. It is clear to everyone who is missing meetings. Sometimes this public record of attendance can be enough to prompt someone into deciding that they really don't have the time and offering their resignation. Either way, it is better for the committee.

Code of conduct

The National Council for Voluntary Organisations (NCVO) has published a code of conduct aimed at trustees working in the voluntary sector. This code draws on the principles of public life laid down by the Nolan Committee.

Step 4: Recruiting volunteers requires a planned approach

Ask any fundraiser what they want the most to make their job easier and they will say 'more volunteers'. They usually follow this with the lament: 'But how do I get them?'

Before you recruit a volunteer ask yourself a number of questions.

Have I got a clear job description?

The first thing to do is to decide what jobs you want done. Before you can successfully attract volunteers you must know what jobs you want them to do and the type of people you're looking for.

Before you write a job description you must ask yourself what the job entails. Be specific. You should not say you want people to help in the fundraising department and send out press releases. Instead, say that the volunteer will fill in donor cards, enter names in the database, address envelopes or talk to other volunteers on the phone.

Why do I want a volunteer?

It is also important to establish why you want a volunteer to do certain tasks and not a paid staff member. You should also ensure that the task is an important one. Volunteers won't stay if they think they are doing jobs that staff won't do.

Do the professional staff really understand the implication of using volunteers?

Sometimes staff think volunteers will make their lives easier by decreasing their workload. They turn up, do the work and go. Unfortunately, there's more to it than that.

First of all, it is a misconception to think that volunteers are a gift to the organisation. They aren't. It takes time and effort to find them, keep them, train them and supervise them. Because they don't get paid, they have to be shown other forms of appreciation and all of this uses staff time, telephone costs and other associated expenses. Staff often underestimate the time needed to give volunteers feedback and appreciation to keep them on board.

Table 7.4 Checklist for designing job description for fundraising and PR volunteer

☐ Is this job really necessary?

☐ Does it fit in with the overall goals and objectives of the dept. or organisation?

☐ Has this job specific tasks?

☐ Can this job be done by a volunteer? Ensure it is not a job more suited to a staff person.

☐ Is there a staff person assigned to supervise and liaise with the volunteers?

☐ Are the procedures/policy of the job clearly written out?

☐ Will doing this job give the volunteer a sense of satisfaction? If not you will have a high turnover of volunteers.

Staff members requesting a volunteer should sit down with the Head of Department and other staff to discuss the questions in Table 7.4 before going through the discipline of filling in a job description like the one in Table 7.5.

Step 5: Recruit volunteers in a professional way

If you approach people in a professional, organised way, potential volunteers will form a good view of you and your organisation.

Target the group or sector you want to approach, e.g. business people. Determine what they are likely to want from volunteering with your organisation. Tailor your request and the volunteer job description to them. In your recruitment material, show the benefit of their working with you.

Choose your volunteers well: screen and select them

You have a duty to select your volunteers very carefully. Paid staff are interviewed and references checked, particularly if they are involved in fundraising. Why would you allow anyone to collect money or be involved in your public relations simply because they have volunteered their time?

It is easy to understand why selection processes may be relaxed. Fundraisers looking for volunteers are often so relieved that someone has volunteered that they forget to screen them.

Fear of interviewing, due to lack of interviewing skills and experience, can also hold you back. The urgency of the situation may dictate the need for volunteers – any volunteers.

Table 7.5 Sample job description for volunteers

NAME

1. JOB TITLE

(e.g. computer and data entry volunteer)

2. STAFF SUPERVISOR – LIAISON

(e.g. Head of Fundraising Dept. – liaise with person running direct mail campaign)

3. NUMBER OF HOURS VOLUNTEERED

(e.g. 4 hours a week)

4. TIME

| office hours | a.m. | 9 – 1 | Monday morning |
| | p.m. | | |

evening

weekend

5. TASKS TO BE PERFORMED

(e.g. input names and addresses into computer)

6. TRAINING

(e.g. Full training in data entry for computer program will be given)

Despite these reasons, screening volunteers is crucial to the long-term success of your programmes.

Screening

The first stage is to screen out those who are totally unsuitable. Writing a clear job description for the volunteer's work helps with this. If the person doesn't have the skills needed they will screen themselves out.

Interviews

The second stage is a face-to-face meeting. To make this easier, list all the things you want to find out in advance. Work through your questions.

A word of caution!

Never be so desperate that you oversell the organisation or overlook some troubling pointers. Be patient and trust your intuition. No volunteer is better than someone unreliable.

Ask the following questions:

☐ Why do you want to volunteer with this organisation?
☐ Why do you want to work in fundraising?
☐ Do you understand the implications of committing your time?

Step 6: Don't throw your volunteers in at the deep end – train them

Are they familiar with the organisation and its work?

Once you have recruited your volunteers you must orient and train them. If the volunteer is going to fundraise for you or be involved in promoting your organisation, they must become very familiar with all aspects of the organisation's work, structures and personnel.

Compile an information pack for every new volunteer. This should include promotional materials, annual reports, sample sponsorship documents, list of branches or local structures.

Introduce them to other staff and make them feel they are appreciated and one of the team. Invite them to press receptions and launches of new products or services. Make sure they receive the regular newsletter. It is an easy way to keep volunteers up to date on evolving projects.

Use experienced volunteers to orient new volunteers. New relationships develop and the more experienced volunteers feel that their skills are appreciated.

Remember how hard it is to recruit new volunteers. Binding volunteers to your organisation and work through training is worth the time it takes.

If your volunteers are going to be working on the telephone or writing letters, it is important to give them appropriate training. Training in telephone techniques greatly enhances a person's productivity.

Support your volunteers – staff supervision of volunteers works

Quite often after volunteers are recruited they are allocated to a set of duties and left to their own devices for long periods. There is no contact or supervision by staff. This can lead to serious problems. It gives the volunteer the message that their work is not high on the staff's agenda. They have no

---

Table 7.6 Good supervision requires that each volunteer

☐ Knows to whom they are reporting.

☐ Has clear instructions. Has someone available to answer questions and give clarification.

☐ Has clearly understood targets.

☐ Is shown appreciation by the staff in tangible ways like – thank you notes, thank you calls or other small tokens.

☐ Receives constructive feedback on tasks accomplished.

---

one to check their progress with and they can feel insecure and unsupported. If a volunteer is going in the wrong direction on a project and is left unsupervised for any length of time, they can be totally off track before anyone notices. This is an excellent way to lose volunteers.

Monitor your volunteers

Monitoring involves keeping track of your volunteers and their work. This is particularly important if you are involved in a large-scale fundraising project and your volunteers are widely dispersed.

The challenge is to find the right balance between too much contact and not enough. Phoning regularly to check is a good way of picking up any problems before they develop. The simple act of asking how everything is going can overcome problems. It's certainly better than trying to find a replacement volunteer midway through a project.

Help your volunteers get formal qualifications

Volunteers often seek some form of formal recognition of the skills they develop in the course of their voluntary work. Recent research by the Wales Council for Voluntary Action found that one third of volunteers wanted formal recognition of their skills.

An initiative by the Institute of Charity Fundraising Managers (ICFM) was launched in 1998. Their Certificate in Fundraising Management will be awarded to a volunteer after assessment based on study, on-the-job work and a report.

Step 7: Recognise and reward your volunteers

Retaining a good volunteer is a headache. 'Burnout' is common among volunteers and staff working in voluntary organisations. This is especially true of fundraising volunteers.

As a fundraiser you need to concentrate on retaining your valuable, experienced volunteer. Giving priority to *volunteer recognition*, both formal and informal, will go a long way to reducing burnout.

Formal recognition includes giving special service prizes and badges, framed certificates or photographs, and invitations to special volunteers dinners or parties. You can nominate one of your volunteers for an award at local or national level for their work with your organisation. You can write about your volunteer's contribution in your newsletter or in articles in local newspapers. Invite a local press photographer to an award ceremony and get your volunteer's photograph in the local newspaper. All of these ideas – and many more that you will think of – tell your volunteers that they are appreciated and that their contribution is formally recognised.

Informal gestures can be just as effective to some volunteers. A genuine thank you at the right moment shows your volunteers that you appreciate them.

Personally encourage your volunteers. Ask them to speak at local clubs or community organisations on your behalf. Invite them to staff meetings, brainstorming sessions, staff parties. Ask their advice about potential fundraising projects before you launch them. They'll know you value their experience in fundraising.

Volunteers, by definition, are unpaid, so they have no salary cheque to reward them. Therefore, it is doubly important that you recognise their motivations and meet them. Volunteers are motivated when they get feedback that their efforts are making a difference.

Step 8: Plan systematic evaluation of your volunteers

As with all projects you run, you will learn from evaluation. Periodically, sit down with your fundraising or PR volunteers and go over the project they have been involved in. Listen to their comments very carefully. Full-time fundraisers can learn an enormous amount from their volunteers. It is important to realise that there are effective and ineffective volunteers – just like paid staff. Regular evaluations of their performance in an informal setting can help you pick up any problems.

When carrying out your evaluation bear the following in mind:

☐ Are they dependable?
☐ Do they turn up on time?
☐ How do they get on with people?
☐ Do they co-operate with other volunteers and staff?
☐ Do they make good ambassadors for the organisation?

Summary points

1. Take stock of your voluntary committees with a view to improving their performance.

2. Be systematic about recruiting new committee members and be clear about their roles.
3. Organise a programme to enhance performance of committee members right through from careful selection to maintenance and recognition.
4. Recruiting fundraising volunteers requires clarity and a planned approach. Write a job description.
5. Recruit volunteers in a professional way.
6. Don't throw your volunteers in at the deep end – train them.
7. Recognise and reward the efforts of volunteers
8. Plan systematic evaluation of your volunteers

8

GET BEYOND THE CONSTRAINTS: KNOW THE REALITIES OF THE FUNDRAISING WORLD

Introduction

In order to get beyond the constraints to fundraising it is important to spend time identifying them. This chapter is by no means a comprehensive list – we can always identify our own brand of constraint – but it highlights some of the major ones: the unpredictable world of fundraising, the decline in household giving, the sometimes hidden but very real costs of fundraising and the insidious negativity with which some members of voluntary organisations approach the process of fundraising.

The unpredictable world of fundraising

The unpredictable, complex and ever-changing nature of fundraising sources today is a constant threat to the sector. The CAF/NAT West survey of 355 organisations in 1996/97 illustrated this. Their findings showed:

1. Although income to the sector from all sources is rising, the funding base is changing and unpredictable. Fifty per cent of respondents to the survey said unpredictability of income was a problem.
2. Complexity of funding sources is another problem. In this survey they found an average of five funding sources per organisation. The smallest ones with income of less than £25,000 had at least two sources of income. The bigger organisations can have up to seven different income sources.
3. Overreliance on one main source of funding was seen as a problem, even though total funding can come from a range of sources.

It is hard to plan a steady increase in your fundraising when faced with such unpredictability and with the need to report to many funders at once. Multiple sources of income can pose problems as each funding source has different application and reporting requirements. Each needs a different approach and this taxes the time and skills of fundraisers, reducing their effectiveness. The other side of the coin is becoming overreliant on one source of funds. This is a risky strategy as you have handed your viability over to one outside source.

Decline in household giving: a major constraint

There has been a decline in the proportion of households giving to not for profits over the last twenty years, from 34 per cent in 1974 to 29 per cent in 1993–94. However, among those who still give, the average real size of their donations has increased. The use of standing orders and direct debits has contributed to this. The increase in size of donations has compensated for the decrease in numbers of donors. Nevertheless the donor base is shrinking. The reasons for this include:

☐ A widening in the gap between different income groups. A fall in income at the lower end could eliminate charitable giving there, while an increase in income at the upper income levels could increase amounts donated there.
☐ Younger people are giving considerably less now than twenty years ago; for example, in the 18–20 age group, giving to charity has dropped from 17 per cent in 1974 of such households to 6 per cent in 1994.
☐ The fact that younger people are giving less and less to charity is a significant pointer for the future funding of the voluntary sector.

Companies supporting charities could give more

Barclays/NGO Finance Charity 100 Index reports that company contributions to charity have remained flat. Why? One reason is that many companies have been through major restructuring and have been forced to look more closely at all their spending. Contributions to voluntary organisations were one of the items cut.

Real costs of fundraising

A constraint to trying new fundraising ideas is the real cost to the organisation of the initiative. This is a crucial guiding principle for every fundraiser.

Recent research done by the Henley Management College with the top 500 charities shows the following interesting results:

☐ The mean income from all fundraising was £5.60 per £1 spent.
☐ Fundraising from trusts was the most cost-effective method.

Negative attitudes as a constraint on fundraisers

Fundraising is not the easiest of professions. Many boards of not for profit organisations have totally unrealistic expectations of fundraisers. Board

Table 8.1 Fundraising costs

Activity	Cost as % of income	Activity	Cost as % of income
Door-to-door collection	102	Direct response TV ads	30
Direct response press ads	58	Direct mail, development	18
Direct mail, recruitment	57	Corporate fundraising	12
Telemarketing	50	Trust fundraising	7

members themselves think direct mail is an intrusion. They don't want people calling them at home and they hate attending special events as they have too many calls on their time. They won't support or get involved in the main types of fundraising, but they expect the fundraiser to achieve targets set by them without any support.

Fundraisers can become demotivated by the firmly held views of some board members. These may include:

'There is no money left'

This block revolves around the idea that there is only a limited amount of money available from donors and it is all already allocated to certain not for profits. In addition there is a feeling that donors are tired of giving and there is no point in asking for more.

This view of the world of fundraising flies in the face of all evidence. There is no limit to the amount available or to the amount a particular donor is likely to give. Experienced and long-time fundraisers know that while individuals often feel supportive of a charity they fail to give money simply because they have not been asked.

'There are too many charities'

This block comes about when fundraisers think that donors give to just one charity. Therefore, if someone regularly donates to a health charity then, according to this view, they won't give to a youth group. People rarely give to just one cause. Always remember that people who donate, do just that – they donate, and often.

'All the good fundraising ideas have been done'

This block is caused when fundraisers take a look at what's happening in their town or city and see lots of high-profile fundraising projects. They believe all the good fundraising ideas have been used up – special events, race meetings, cake sales, have all been done to death. They forget their client base, their existing donors, their volunteers. What is happening is their realisation of how hard fundraising actually is.

Every fundraiser should be aware of their real value in fundraising. You alone cannot raise the organisation's fundraising target. Don't let anyone try to persuade you otherwise. Fundraising must involve people at all levels of the organisation. The fundraiser is the strategist, the planner, the facilitator, the motivator and above all the person who thanks everyone.

Fundraisers' nightmare people

Fundraisers have to be extremely focused people. They must be good planners and be good at getting results. Fundraisers more than most professions are judged on specific targets and results. Because of the focus on results and the importance of the funds to the financial well-being of the organisation, fundraisers have to be very careful about the type of people who are involved in their fundraising work and avoid the following.

All talk/no action people

You'll recognise them as the people who promise everything – sell tickets, contact musicians, write letters, send out information – but never deliver anything. They are a negative influence on your work. You'll recognise them soon enough. They are the ones always leaving or returning from trips, always at meetings and they tend to have the nastiest 'gatekeeper' secretaries. Allow them to promise, by all means, but have your own deadlines and be prepared to draw a line when they pass. Forget them.

Negative people

'That idea will never work' is their watchword. You'll recognise them because they always resist change and new ideas. Fundraising requires creativity and enthusiasm. Negative people pull the whole fundraising effort down. You'd be better off without them.

Let's cut back on activities people

Some people masquerade as contributors to the board or fundraising committee. Examine their record over the years and you'll find that they have never made a single contribution or attempted to solicit one. Yet these people are always first to propose rationalisation and cutbacks. They need to be replaced by people who can and do fundraise. This may seem obvious, but can be overlooked.

It is important to keep a positive outlook so I'm including in this chapter

Table 8.2 Sixteen ways to overcome constraints on fundraisers

---

1. Keep trying things
Don't give up. Always try something new – one gift a week, one new event a month, whatever – keep moving.

2. Ready, steady, go
Remember the 'go' part. Many fundraisers get stuck on the planning and analysing stages.

3. Read everything
Fundraising ideas come from everywhere. Read every magazine you can get your hands on. Go to libraries. Read books – especially business, self-improvement and sales and marketing ones. Fundraising is a business activity and you can get wonderful ideas from these sectors.

4. Be open-minded when recruiting fundraisers – staff and voluntary
Recruit from as broad a pool as possible. Don't always look for people with experience in fundraising. People in sales and marketing, young business people all have the necessary attributes.

5. Delegate and give responsibility to others
Don't feel you have to do everything yourself. If you do you'll reduce the work to the speed at which you work.

6. Always be in training
Attend seminars, lectures, training courses. There are always guest lecturers at the marketing institute, public relations institute and elsewhere. Look in the newspapers, trade journals and magazines.

7. Radiate passion and enthusiasm
People react positively to enthusiasm. They get caught up in it.

8. Use your time well
Concentrate on doing the productive things first and remember not to confuse activity with results.

9. Fundraising is a risky business so be prepared to take risks
You must be prepared to trust your instincts and back innovative projects.

10. Seek out optimists
Mixing with optimistic people keeps you positive. Make it a practice to avoid negative people, especially burnt-out fundraisers who look at every new idea with scepticism.

11. Meet people
Make appointments, follow up contacts. Get out and meet people face to face. Ask for money, for help, for their time. Don't hide behind your desk or your plans.

12. Ask, ask, ask
Again and again fundraisers are told that if they had not asked for the gift they would not have received it.

13. Identify your top ten potential major donors
Learn everything you can about them. Keep this list with you at all times. Work on it. This is where your biggest results will come from. Work out how they are going to be approached. Then approach them.

14. Work with teams – not committees
Teams have plans, objectives and team spirit. Committees have meetings, agendas and spend hours taking, reading and discussing 'minutes'.

15. Rise above the humdrum
Allocate a minimum of an hour every week to thinking. Don't get bogged down in the day-to-day aspects of fundraising. Don't get totally overtaken by one big fundraising campaign. Always keep your brain creative. Schedule brainstorming time.

16. Finally – ask questions all the time
Constantly query how you do things and why you do them. Don't get complacent about your fundraising approach. Keep questioning it.

on constraints a set of well tried ways of overcoming setbacks and remaining positive and motivated.

Constraint: your attitude to fundraising

Fundraising begins with your realising that the work you and your organisation are doing is worthwhile. If you are not clear on that point, fundraising will be difficult for you. Be clear that the good things that your organisation are doing are equal to the money funding them. Remember: without fundraising your work will not happen.

Fear of asking for money

One of the roles of a good fundraiser is to enable those around them to conquer their fear of asking for money. This involves understanding fears and hang-ups, then realising that this fear is normal. It happens in all organisations at some time. The most important step is working with the board and volunteers to overcome these personal fears. If you do this, you will have gained a corps of effective fundraisers.

Fundraisers who are realistic, recognise these fears and take positive steps to overcome them instead of shouldering all the responsibilities of fundraising themselves are ultimately the most effective fundraisers.

Fundraisers have to be good psychologists. They have to understand what makes people tick. They have to be realistic about who will work or contribute and who won't. The fundraiser's attitude to 'passengers' is crucial to their success. Sometimes the hard option – of facing people with their non-performance – may be the only one to take. People's feelings can be hurt and the fundraiser has to be able to deal with that, without causing offence.

Your attitude should be that your responsibility is to the organisation's donors and to the people you are serving. Your volunteers and donors need constant thanks, but the people who hold back the organisation, who won't fundraise, who won't let others fundraise, who constantly criticise and gripe, may need to be replaced. Good fundraisers often face difficult decisions about people.

A phrase I always remember from a chairman of a national organisation to his board was straight to this core point. It goes like this: 'As members of the board of this voluntary organisation, we're here to give, get or get off.'

Fundraising is not begging

If your co-workers or volunteers feel that your organisation should focus exclusively on its programmes and let someone else do the fundraising, you are in trouble. You are probably experiencing the *fundraising is begging syndrome*. This attitude is more common than many organisations admit to. It is important to be clear that fundraising is definitely **not** begging. Fundraising provides an opportunity for people to contribute tangibly to something of value in their community or to make something of importance happen.

No one gives to a negative person

Many people approach fundraising tentatively, anticipating a no. They'll say, 'I'm sorry to bother you ...' or 'I know you get asked all the time, but ...'. The underlying belief is that people don't care about what your organisation is doing and that your fundraising is not going to work. This negative wish can be self-fulfilling. If people sense your negativity, they will respond negatively. Look around you; are your co-workers, volunteers, members of your fundraising committee, positive and enthused? If not, focus on changing their attitude or replacing them with people who are.

Commitment wins donors

If your fundraisers are committed to your organisation and its work, that attitude will shine through. To be committed they must understand what you do and believe in it. Ensure that everyone fundraising for your organisation is thoroughly briefed on your mission statement, your reason for existing and the services you provide.

Your organisation exists to fill a need

Not for profits exist to fill a need, be it providing housing for people with special needs or counselling for parents of chronically ill children. Businesses and for profits stimulate need by marketing and advertising, and then respond to that need. Not for profits don't have to stimulate need. It's out there and they are trying to respond to it. If you are clear on this it will greatly help you when approaching someone for funds.

Summary points

1. Fundraising operates in a highly unpredictable world.
2. There is a decline in household giving over time.
3. Companies could give more to charity.
4. The real costs of fundraising should be taken into account when reporting results.
5. There are real but unrecognised difficulties in being a fundraiser at present.
6. Negative attitudes are a constraint to fundraisers. Be aware of them.
7. Know and understand the typical fundraiser's nightmare people.
8. Work on your attitude – having the right attitude to fundraising is vital.
9. Overcome the real fear of fundraisers – the fear of asking for money.

Part 2

USE THESE SIX SUCCESSFUL WAYS TO FUNDRAISE

Introduction

No one organisation will use all the fundraising techniques available. Larger organisations with a dedicated fundraising or development department will cover many of them and will draw income from a variety of sources. However, small organisations may have to rely on one source of income. In reality, many small organisations are totally reliant on raising income from the general public in quite unsophisticated ways.

Before we begin discussing the practicalities of different types of fundraising, it is worthwhile to consider the seven rules for fundraisers, which will lead to greater success no matter what type of fundraising you embark on.

The seven rules for fundraisers

Rule 1: Believe in your organisation

Every fundraiser must believe that the work of their organisation is worthwhile before they begin their fundraising activities. If the organisation fills a need and does it well, they will be able to show that the money raised translates into real benefits to the community.

Unfortunately, some not for profits feel that their very existence and their desire to save the world is enough. Often, administrators or project officers do not see the need to co-operate with the fundraiser. They can cut the fundraiser out of the picture. They feel people should simply contribute to their cause. Fundraising in such an organisation is almost impossible.

Rule 2: Good fundraisers always find the donor's self-interest

You are asking for money. Your success depends on realising that people give money for different reasons. You must understand what these reasons are. Why do different people give money? What motivates them? What would they really like in return for their donation? Do they like recognition, publicity, personal thanks or something else? In all aspects of life people do things if they think they are personally important to them. Parting with money is no different. They will give, if you convince them that it is important to them to do so. Knowing this, you can see why it is so important to individualise and personalise all your communications with your potential donors. Take the time to get names, addresses, and titles correct. Do not write the easy 'Dear Friend', or worse still 'Dear Supporter'.

Take the time to write personal notes or personal postscripts. Count the number of times you use the words you and I in your letters. If you are really thinking about your donor, the important word should be 'you' and the word 'I' should vanish from the text.

Rule 3: Good fundraisers are always courteous

Courtesy is caring enough to treat people with care and respect – treating others as you would wish to be treated. Good manners and courtesy are essential for fundraisers. They are basically common sense and respect for others. Always, always thank people. Thank donors, thank volunteers who give of their time – but remember also to thank the not so obvious people: staff who worked late for you, venue staff who came in early, especially for you, Red Cross or first aid volunteers who gave up their free time. Thank them personally, but also let their boss know. Do it in writing.

I remember a well-known circus which helped with the press launch of a nationwide fundraising campaign. They pulled out all the stops and gave us all their acts for free. We gave each member of the cast a gift later on in the day, we wrote to the owner of the circus, we put their name on all press materials and we gave them photos and a video of their contribution for their own public relations. They were stunned. No one had thanked them before. They helped the same organisation for years afterwards.

Rule 4: Good fundraisers are good salespeople

All fundraisers are selling something. You are selling your programme, your tickets or your gala night. Realising this can be very encouraging for a fundraiser because selling is a long way from begging.

Any salesperson will tell you the key to selling is finding the customers for your products or service, and then selling the benefits to them. Promote your services and how they will personally benefit the person. Talk to sales people about their techniques, read 'how to' sales books. They'll teach you how to accentuate the positive and many other attributes of good sales people.

Rule 5: Good fundraisers are always prepared

Do not miss an opportunity. You never know when one of the people or organisations you have approached for a donation will respond to you. So be prepared with a minimum amount of basic materials at all times.

Know your organisation's work

Know your organisation's work at all levels and have it available in easily read, human-interest style. Have your statistics ready.

Be ready to meet people

Be prepared to meet people at a moment's notice. If a potential donor or the chair of a fundraising committee can only meet you on Saturday morning be prepared to go then.

Be ready to produce sponsorship proposals

Be prepared to work on a sponsorship deal at short notice. Sometimes following a successfully publicised event, a commercial company may approach you as they think your organisation will fit in well with their plans. If you have a good, well-planned fundraising programme in place you can respond promptly.

Practise your sales speech

If you are unsure about how to approach person-to-person meetings with donors or sponsors, do your homework well and practise. The most difficult part in the meeting is asking for money. Many fundraisers make great speeches about their organisation's work because they are on sure ground, but fail to close the deal for fear of asking for the money. Practise what you are going to say. If possible, do a role play with a friend or colleague. Get them to play the part of a reluctant donor and practise your approach until you are totally at ease with it.

Ask for advice

Get as much advice as possible. Ask other fundraisers, board members, professionals in different fields. If you are approaching a major retail chain for sponsorship in kind, talk to people in the retail trade, journalists, PR people and staff of major retail chains. Find out what interests them. People love being asked for advice.

Rule 6: Good fundraisers always evaluate

Fundraisers should never lose an opportunity to learn from their past projects and so should always evaluate each fundraising project. This is particularly important for people new to fundraising. They may have just started on a small project and done well and will want to talk about the success before moving on to a bigger one. Evaluation does not have to be a witchhunt.

Rule 7: Good fundraisers paint word-pictures

When you are talking about your organisation's activities you must attract people's attention and keep it. You have to appeal to their emotions and needs. An effective way to do this is to talk about human beings. Explain your programme and services in human terms. Do not say 'We ran 24 education programmes for disadvantaged young women' or 'We have six drop-in shelters for drug addicts' . That is the language you use when you send in your annual report to the local government funding agency.

Describe your activities in terms of the changes in real people's lives in your community. Say Alice and Fumi were very young mothers on the edge of permanent drug use, feeling worthless and unable to support themselves. Through attending our drop-in centre and progressing to part-time classes, while using our crèche, they are now working part-time, supporting themselves and beginning to take charge of their lives. This shows that your organisation makes a real difference to people's lives.

9

SPECIAL EVENTS: HOW TO MAKE MONEY AND HAVE FUN

Introduction

The first thing to be said about special events is that they are the least efficient way to raise money. They demand lots of staff time, use up volunteers and can be very exhausting. On the other hand, they are exciting, stimulating, fun and attract a lot of attention to your organisation and its work. By all means stage them, but be careful where you fit them into your fundraising plan. In addition, be sensible about how many you undertake in any one year.

If your board or fundraising committee equates fundraising with special events, then it can be difficult to get them to spend money on setting up direct mail or any other programme. Attractive as these events are from a PR point of view, they will never build a cost-efficient, reliable fundraising programme.

Deciding whether to stage a special event

If your only goal is to make money, a special event may not be the most effective way to go about it. Your fundraising committee might be better off getting involved in a major donor campaign. That way they begin at once and you have no financial risks. If you need money immediately to keep the doors of your organisation open, a special event is not for you. It is too time-consuming and financially risky.

You must know at which specific target group you are aiming the event. Themed events appeal to a younger group, award dinners appeal to business people, film premières to the celebrity and society set! A good indication of success is if your first meeting can be certain of pre-selling to a certain percentage of the guest list or have a large number of committee members committed to selling tickets.

A key factor in your decision will be if you have a good working committee, led by an enthusiastic chairperson, to sell the tickets or tables. If you do not, do not take it on. As a fundraiser, you could organise the event but you could never reach the sales target single-handed.

Choosing the right event

A clear set of goals is needed to guarantee the 'right' event. The right event is one that fits well with the ethos of the organisation and is going to make money. The 'special' in the special event is usually supplied by the energy, commitment and imagination of a small group of people who form the organising committee. Because an event uses up so much volunteer time and goodwill you have to be sure that the one you choose is worth the time and trouble.

Everyone must be clear on the overall budget and the target net return after all costs are met. If you are making less than 50 per cent return it may need a rethink. Spending £100,000 to stage a giant gala party only to make £20,000 for the organisation is a bad use of resources. You might decide to run something less exotic and less costly in terms of outgoings.

Common types of events

In selecting the right event it is important to decide on the reason why you are running it. Some of the most common objectives are:

☐ to make a profit
☐ to attract new members
☐ to boost morale of staff and volunteers
☐ to provide information
☐ to gain great publicity
☐ to give recognition to donors or volunteer workers

It is essential before you embark on your special event to clarify which of these objectives you have in mind. Then draw up your plan to achieve that objective.

Here are some examples of special events which have different objectives, not always to raise funds.

1. Existing donor events

This kind of event suits organisations with an established list of donors who could give more but are not doing so. You have a ready-made audience so the challenge is to catch their attention, get them to come along and gently let them know about the organisation and how much it values them. Your event could be a special donor reception, an art event or special celebrity evening.

2. Annual fundraising campaign parties

If you have an annual fundraising campaign which is becoming a little jaded you could kick-start it with a big party. You could also hold a special party for one specialised constituency like the financial community. If you do not often bring your donors or supporters together, this can be successfully done once or twice.

3. 'Target new groups' event

All not for profits have to seek out new constituencies if they are to survive. If you have been supported by one group which is now dwindling in number you need to reach out to different groups, e.g. if stay-at-home mothers were your mainstay, perhaps you should follow changing trends and target working mothers and young professional women. Hold a young businesswomen's evening or lunch.

4. Sponsored events

If the sponsor puts up most of the money and provides hands-on help by way of people, these events can be a great gift. However, a word of caution – make sure your organisation is happy with the sponsoring company. In addition, make sure they are not using your organisation to put an altruistic shine on their event and expecting you to do all the work.

5. Business-led events

Sometimes a company may decide to support a not for profit by running an event especially geared to its own constituency. Examples include a publisher launching a book, a restaurant hosting an evening to publicise its new menu, or a special sales evening at a department store.

6. A 'free' evening

A not for profit may organise an event and charge no admission. These are usually aimed at supporters or donors. They can often yield surprising amounts due to the amount of goodwill they generate. Having a circus perform free for you and then inviting all your donors to bring along a child can do wonders in spreading goodwill towards your organisation. You will get the reputation of not always looking for something.

7. Targeted audience events

These events are targeted at specific sectors of the community. A good example is a sports dinner held on the night before a big game, for example, a dinner featuring speakers from the international rugby world held on the eve of a major international rugby game.

This event can be sold with relative ease to members of rugby clubs and business people with a known interest in the sport. This event can be chaired by a well-known rugby player who will open all the right doors.

8. Recognition events

An excellent way to get access to new supporters is to link your charity with a well-known name by way of a testimonial dinner. Have your organisation give an 'award of excellence' or 'civic person of the year' award to a celebrity or civic leader. You can attract your dinner guests from well-wishers. If you choose someone from a field quite different from the one your organisation is operating in, you will gain access to a whole range of new people.

9. Celebrity events

Celebrate your anniversary, your foundation day, the birthday of your founder, the opening of your new clinic or programme. Find a reason to mark the passing of a significant event or the winning of an award. Business and political leaders like to be associated with success in the community – it reflects well on them. You can gather a good attendance and gain media attention.

Table 9.1 Essential elements for financial success of a special event

---

☐ A hardworking committee willing to actually sell.

☐ A good lead-in time to ensure adequate time for logistical arrangements and a long selling time.

☐ Good financial controls, realistic targets and a clear knowledge of the break-even point, i.e., when tickets sold cover all expenses and from the next sale on you are making a profit. You must be clear on this because if you do not reach the break-even point you may have to cancel the event to avoid a financial loss.

☐ Advance knowledge of who makes up your potential market. You need to have the comfort of knowing that on your first selling day, you know 25–35 per cent of the tickets are pre-sold.

☐ A detailed plan of action covering marketing, sales, public relations, volunteers, logistics. Once you have laid this out, then no matter how unwieldy your committee is they can progress through the plan.

10. 'Concentric circles' events

These are events which start small with a circle of supporters, who in turn involve another circle and so on until the event grows to a huge regional or national event. The Irish Hospice movement ran a coffee morning in association with a well-known coffee retailer based on this principle. It ended up with virtually everyone in the Republic of Ireland drinking coffee on one morning in the autumn generating a sizeable income for the Hospice movement.

The first year of any major special event

Do not contemplate doing a major special event unless it is repeatable in some form for a number of years. The first event is always a trial run. You learn by your mistakes and collect lots of names and addresses for the second year. You should ensure that you get lots of publicity for the first event. So concentrate on angles which will interest the press. This will help you maximise returns for less work in the second and subsequent years.

Special events: ideal for public relations

Whatever anyone might say about special events being time-consuming and hard on staff and volunteers, no one can say that they are not good for publicity. If handled properly, special events can be an excellent boost to an organisation's PR calendar.

Table 9.2 Fundraising costs

☐ Never give away free tickets without a very good reason. It lessens the impact of your event. Make sure all staff and fundraising volunteers know and appreciate why you are doing this.

☐ Never expect volunteers to do things without thanks. Give them a good dinner or seats in a special screening of a film première. Introduce them to the star of the evening.

☐ Never lose your temper. Never lose your cool. If you do, it could be the end of the smooth running of the event.

☐ Never allocate yourself specific tasks on the night. Delegate everything. Then you're free to oversee the whole event and to deal with the horrendous problem, that always appears five minutes before the start: the guest of honour is late, your master of ceremonies has not turned up, the press are out of control, whatever. I'm sure you've had your own private nightmare.

Table 9.3 Special events: things you always do

☐ Have a detailed plan.

☐ Pay extraordinary attention to details.

☐ Walk the ground, once, twice, three times.

☐ Go though the schedule for the evening at the venue. Act like a guest, drive in, park your car, check in your coat, and so on, through the entire schedule until you leave at the end of the night. This way you will uncover all the hidden problems like only one person checking coats and you're expecting 500 people to arrive within a 10-minute period.

☐ Walk all your volunteers though the schedule at the venue. You can't be everywhere, so if they are asked questions they must know the answers. If they have been thoroughly briefed on site they will be more effective on the night.

☐ Double-check everything and confirm by fax or a letter.

☐ View everything personally, for example, the chairs, tables, flower arrangements, public address system – everything. Do not take suppliers' word for it. It is no good if all the chairs for your guests are plastic and you're charging £1,500 a table. You do not want to discover this on the night.

☐ Ask to taste the food and the wine in advance. Get a second opinion.

☐ Give copies of the detailed, timed, schedule to everyone working with you.

☐ Remember someone must be the boss – that someone knows everything. They do not do everything but they sure know what everyone else is doing.

☐ PLAN, PLAN, PLAN.

☐ Thank everyone regularly.

A practical guide to running a black tie award dinner

This is a stylish, gala dinner held somewhere exclusive or unusual, at which you serve excellent food and wine and charge way above the odds. It is important to have a good reason for the people to attend. They won't just come to dinner; the kinds of people who go to these dinners have more invitations than time. Money is not a big issue; their time and boredom levels are.

You must find a reason to engage their interest. There are many different ways, but some tried-and-tested ones are: to give an award to a leader in your community or to celebrate an anniversary in your organisation's history. Invent an award and call it the '[Name of Your Organisation] Award of Excellence.'

Choosing the person to be honoured at an award dinner

From a fundraising viewpoint there are crucial ground-rules for choosing the person. Do not make the mistake of simply choosing someone who is worthy of the award – choose someone with connections and a circle of business contacts who will buy tables at your dinner. Remember: your prime objective is fundraising, which in this instance translates into table sales.

When you have got the person's agreement, involve their family or a close business associate at the earliest planning stage. They will help you draw up a list of companies to approach for table sales. You normally approach their financial, legal, marketing and public relations companies, and other major service providers.

At one award dinner for a prominent businessman representatives of each of the business sectors in which he was involved bought tables. They covered the hotel and restaurant sector, the electrical business, both whole-sale and retail, and the newspaper business.

Do your research

If you research the person's hobbies and interests well and build these into the schedule, you can build a special and memorable evening. You may discover a media figure who admires the person and will act as master of ceremonies. You could ask their favourite restaurant to do the catering – they will give you a good price in exchange for the publicity. Approach a major jeweller or glass company to commission a special piece for the award. Promise lots of publicity and status associated with their piece being presented to a well-known business person.

Allow adequate lead-in time

Getting the right person is crucial, so give yourself plenty of time. You should be making initial contact at least 12 months in advance; 18 months is better. Book your venue and continue your research. Get your planning committee together six months in advance. Make sure everyone on the committee knows that they have to sell tables. You can't afford non-working passengers.

Send out your preliminary letters 16 weeks in advance and prepare for hard work from 12 weeks onwards.

Hire a graphic designer and select a theme for all your printed materials. It could be cream paper with navy-blue print and a gold embossed logo. Use this for the notepaper. Pay attention to details – cloth tablecloths touching the floor, abundant flowers in one or two colours. Get a blow-up photograph of the person and put it behind the podium. Put a spotlight on it.

Ask for expert help with the choice of wine. Approach wine wholesalers and explain that you need excellent wine for an exclusive group. You'll find that they prefer to sell you expensive wine at lower prices than give you cheaper wine free. The kinds of people who attend these events are their dream customers – wine merchants want them to sample their expensive wines.

Finally, research your award recipient well and you'll build an excellent event around your findings.

Summary points

1. Be clear about the real costs of a special event before you start.
2. Be realistic about expected income.
3. Choose your event with great care. Time spent on research is worthwhile.
4. Know the things you 'never do' and the things you 'always do' when running a special event.
5. Plan your Black Tie Award Dinner with care, especially the choice of person to be honoured.

BUILDING RELATIONSHIPS: DIRECT MAILING, MAJOR DONORS, BEQUESTS

Introduction

One of the most important aspects of fundraising is to build a relationship with your donors. Like most relationships, it starts with a short interaction (the general inquiry or small one-off donation) and progresses from there. The depth of the relationship and how it progresses is in your hands.

A commonly held view is that relationship fundraising develops from one-off donations through regular and increasing donations up to the level of being mentioned in the donor's will. This progression can be envisaged as follows:

General public → Specific inquiry → Donation → Regular donor → Major donor → Wills

This chapter explores the different elements of that progression. First, direct mail will allow you to identify donors through 'cold or prospect mailings'. Then, through a refinement of your direct mail approach using 'donor retention mailings', you develop and maintain a link with a smaller number of donors turning them into regular donors. You then plan to cultivate a small number of people who will give you large donations and become 'major donors'. The final stage is to encourage people to leave your organisation some money in their will. This section will help you understand the general elements of this approach and take you through the practicalities of each stage.

Your relationship is with people

Fundamental to building relationships in fundraising is the recognition that it's people who give donations and make wills. So all of your approaches must put people first. Also, people have needs, desires and wants. So to develop a good relationship with them you must find out what these are and cater for them. When you have developed a relationship you must then work at maintaining it. At best it is fragile – only as strong as your last contact. Once up and going you have to avoid taking the relationship for granted.

Always thank people. I feel so strongly about this that I've included a full chapter on donor recognition in this book (chapter 6). Be honest and transparent in all your dealings with donors. Tell them if things are going wrong. They could possibly help you in some significant way.

You're in the 'people business' now

Direct mail, major donor programmes and legacy campaigns are all techniques of contacting people and earning valued money for your organisation. Handled properly, all these techniques are acceptable to people. However, here is the challenge – to carry these out effectively (in terms of income generation) while being sensitive to people's needs.

Donors often say that they were pleased to be approached. They might not have given without the request. However, many donors – or more importantly non-donors -complain about *how* they were approached or treated. Their reactions are primarily personal. They felt offended by too brash an approach, they were upset by a failure to thank them or they took exception to being asked to join the organisation when they had been loyal donors for five years.

Putting people first, means adopting a certain work ethnic. This can be demanding. It means putting your donor before your staff and yourself. In practical terms, it means answering phone calls and letters promptly, paying great attention to details and devoting time to personal thank yous.

Direct mail

Direct mail opens up a wonderful range of opportunities. However, it is essential to realise that there is a lot more to direct mail than stuffing things into envelopes and sending them to the post office. Despite the wide range of fundraising ideas around, most charitable donations are still solicited and delivered by post.

According to the Direct Marketing Association (UK) 2,370 million items of direct mail were sent in 1994. This represented a growth of 230 per cent since 1984. However, the UK still receive one of the lowest numbers of direct mail pieces per capita in Europe.

Do not start direct mail until you fully understand it

Many people involved in not for profits, particularly people involved in small-scale or local fundraising, can have a negative attitude to direct mail.

Quite often they do not understand it. They see it as junk mail and frequently say 'Doesn't everyone hate junk mail?'

Before you begin to introduce direct mail into your organisation make sure you fully understand the whole process and the thinking behind it. You will need to educate your board and your more traditional fundraising volunteers and staff. You would not buy an expensive car without some advice, so do not commit your organisation's budget without a thorough investigation.

The first step is to establish if this approach will suit your organisation. Then explore how the process works and the importance of building donors over time. Talk to other not for profits which have successful direct mail programmes. Consult the Direct Mail Association.

The role of individual giving is crucial to the voluntary sector. Not only does it supply income but it is an indicator of solid support for the organisation. In the CAF Nat West study of voluntary organisations carried out in 1996, one third of the organisations surveyed said that money from individual donations was the most important source of income for them.

Individual donations are particularly important to smaller charities, i.e. income less than £25,000. Resources suggest that for incomes of less than £100,000 it could be approximately one quarter of income. CAF's top 500 fundraising charities derive half of their funds from voluntary income, of which half comes from individual giving.

A number of surveys have been carried out in recent years to find that useful indicator – the 'average individual giving to charity per month'. Although figures vary, CAF has concluded that it lies in the range between £8.30 and £10.30 per month.

Consult the experts

When you are ready to get involved in direct mail you can then get expert advice. Talk to the myriad number of companies involved in this area. If you require advice or literature about direct marketing contact the Direct Marketing Association of the UK. You might even consider joining the Association.

Fundamentals of direct mail

Direct mail fundraising is for the long term. Amazingly, charities came third behind financial services and motor insurance in the UK direct mail market which was worth £1,135 million in 1995.

A crucial influence over any fundraiser is whether they are fundraising for immediate survival or building a long-term fundraising base for the future. If you are lucky enough to be building for the future then you should consider direct mail.

Three fundamental points are worth considering at this point:

1. Get and keep a donor

Many business people believe that they need to focus primarily on creating customers rather than on making money. Fundraisers can learn from this approach. Direct mail fundraising focuses on getting customers or donors with whom, over time, you develop a long-term donation relationship. You do not focus on the money first – a surprising thought for fundraisers.

2. Relationship-building

The approach to the donor is personal – one to one. You learn more about your donor and in the process they learn more about you.

3. Databases

A fundamental element of direct mail is the building and use of databases. So when you embark on this make sure you have involved someone who is skilled in this area, either in-house or involving an outside expert.

Know your AIDA

Increasingly, not for profit organisations are setting up direct mail programmes as a way of generating a steady and growing donor base. Although people complain about the volume of post they receive they continue to contribute in large numbers to appeals by mail.

The AIDA concept explains how this works. It is based on four principles:

1. Grab Attention
2. Interest People
3. Generate Desire
4. Prompt Action

Attention

First, your outer envelope must get the person's attention so that they want to open it. Then the opening lines of your letter, combined with the graphics, must hold their attention long enough so that it stays out of the rubbish bin.

Interest

You have their attention now, the package/letter must present something of interest to the reader.

Desire

They are now interested, but your package must generate a desire to give.

Action

Finally, if your direct mail package has done its job, a small percentage of recipients will decide to make a contribution. Now your package must overcome their inertia and move them to action, i.e. sending a cheque and returning the prepaid envelope.

Cold and warm mailings

Direct mail campaigns commonly divide into the donor acquisition phase (cold mailings) and the donor renewal phase (warm mailings). In the first, you mail large numbers of people and plan to get a certain percentage return. This is usually quite low. These are your new donors. You build on that small donor base and develop a relationship with those donors. At the same time you keep sending out cold mailings with the aim of gradually building up your donor base.

The elements of a direct mail campaign

1. An effective message

An effective message is one that motivates the recipient to become a donor to your organisation. No one, no matter how good, happens on this magical message the first time out. A lot of experimenting or testing is needed and most importantly the ability to learn from mistakes.

You can do a sample mailing to a small number of people and test different things; you can test the copy or content of the letter, the style of the letter or different signatories. By careful analysis of yields and controlling the variables you will work out what makes up the most effective message. Then mail that to a larger number of people.

2. Components of direct mail package

When designing your direct mail package you should approach it as a unified campaign. Choose a theme which runs through all elements of the package – for example, colours, logo and style of print.

You are free to put almost anything in your package, but if you are

---

Table 10.1 The elements of a successful direct mail campaign

☐ An effective message.

☐ Well put together campaign.

☐ A carefully targeted mailing list.

Table 10.2 Typical elements of direct mail package

The envelope
Direct mail fundraising tends to consist of a number of items within an envelope rather than a flyer or catalogue.

The letter
The letter is generally long, 2–3 pages. Testing has proved that potential donors want to read all about the organisation and like to see a long letter.

The reply device
This can be on a card, slip of paper or full page. It should have the prospect's name and address and recap the fundraising proposal, e.g., 'I want to contribute to the fight to find a cure for AIDS'. Average pledge amounts should be given.

The reply envelope
A return-addressed reply envelope. You can pre-pay the postage if you can afford it.

The brochure
This can supplement the information in your letter.

The testimonial
This can be in the form of a message or note from a beneficiary of the organisation's services or a celebrity.

The PS
Research has shown that people often read the PS first. So make it concise and say what you want.

---

starting from scratch you should get some professional advice. There are companies and consultants who specialise in this. Certain elements have evolved over years of direct mail testing.

Do not use your general fundraising brochure. It has been shown that they don't help raise funds.

The style of the letter is very important. It should be like a personal note, not a business letter. Ensure someone good at this type of informal style writes the letter or get professional help. Keep sentences short and simple. Use short words and keep paragraphs between 5 and 6 lines. If your letter is full of dense, complicated paragraphs it will go straight in the bin.

You should try to make the envelope as interesting as possible, make the letter look like a 'real letter' and make it as readable as you can. The whole package should look good, but not too expensive.

3. A good list

No matter how emotive your message and how well presented your materials, if they are sent to the wrong people you won't reach your target.

Direct mail fundraising can succeed or fail depending on the quality of the list.

List selection requires considerable care. If you are using your organisation's own list remember that it will be out of date after about six months. The same applies when using lists from directories or membership lists.

When compiling a list remind yourself of the fundamental point of direct mail, which is to make a personal approach, one to one, to a potential donor. The better you know the person, the more appropriate you can make your message. So spend time compiling a list of people you consider most likely to respond positively to your organisation.

Three guidelines will help:

1. Lists from outside sources.
2. Your own list will give you better results.
3. Try to buy or rent lists as similar to your own as possible.

It stands to reason that people who know your organisation and its value will be more likely to support you financially than someone who has never heard of you.

Analysis improves your lists. Constant analysis of returns from different lists will enable you to see the characteristics of people who give and those who do not. This is valuable as it helps you cut down on wasteful mailings.

Testing

Rule number one is – do not test two variables at the same time. Basically, you can either do tests of new lists or new approaches. You should not test a new letter or new copy with a new list. You won't know which worked. When you test a new copy, make sure you test it against your proven package. Do it at the same time to remove the variable of timing.

There is a good deal to the area of testing. Ensure that you learn as much as you can. It really will enhance your results. No matter how much you test, remember: testing is an indication not a promise of results.

Never lose an opportunity to collect names for your list

Think about how many people come in contact with your organisation on a daily basis. They buy tickets at your office or library, attend your information day. They know your work and have an interest in it. Get everyone who deals with 'clients' to record their names and addresses. Obviously, use common sense about whether you think these are potential donors or not.

List rental

If you do not have a list of your own you can rent one. Tread carefully when entering into this and get expert help. There are so many variables and

---

Table 10.3 Key points for successful direct mail letters

☐ People give to people. So put the 'people element' up front in your appeal.

☐ Be precise about what you need. Tell them what you can achieve with their money.

☐ Generate a sense of urgency. People give money when they see a real and immediate need. Use a deadline date.

☐ Use emotional language. You must make a link between the donor and recipient of the money. You must cast the appeal in language that will engage the donor's emotions.

☐ Use a case history. Write about a moving story or someone your organisation has helped. Make it vivid, real and appealing.

---

things that can go wrong, from renting inappropriate names, to getting the prepared lists full of duplications, to paying two sets of commission to the list broker and list manager. Contact the Direct Marketing Association for help.

Key points for successful direct mail letters

Keep people reading

☐ Don't use three words if you can say it in one.
☐ Do not use complicated words – keep it simple.
☐ Keep the reader reading by using link words like 'also', 'moreover', 'and'.
☐ Ask questions at the beginning and the end of paragraphs to get people's interest.
☐ Use short sentences – 16 words or less.
☐ Use short paragraphs and keep to one point per paragraph.

Remember why you are doing direct mail – to get donations and have a look at the following pointers to increasing your yield

How to avoid your direct mail being treated as junk mail

You will have heard many detractors of direct mail refer to it as junk mail. They feel there is too much of it and it is unwelcome. A recent survey of charities showed 18 per cent of them were concerned that direct mail could too often be seen as junk mail.

So what is junk mail? It is widely regarded as any kind of unsolicited mail. There is a school of thought which says that it is carelessness and lack of planning which results in far too much misdirected mail arriving on your

Table 10.4 Pointers to enhance your yield

☐ Always remember to ask for a specific amount of money.

☐ Ask for a big amount – you might get it.

☐ State the problem, show there is a solution and make the reader realise they can be a part of that solution.

☐ Write person to person.

☐ State clearly the purpose for which the money will be used.

doorstep (literally!), followed closely by inaccurate and badly maintained lists.

No one minds getting a certain level of mail, but what infuriates people is when they get five letters from one organisation all addressed to variations of their name. It is vital you avoid this. You do not want to irritate your potential donors by burying them in inaccurately addressed letters. People are very sensitive about the way their name is spelt, so always check this first.

Direct mail link to public relations

There is a large public relations element to direct mail so it is important not to detract from the image of your organisation by appearing to be inefficient or wasteful by sending too many letters to one person or to members of the same family.

Control your costs or perish

The success of your direct mail campaign in the start-up phase will be closely influenced by how tightly you control your costs. When sourcing for your printing, packaging or posting take advantage of the competitive nature of the industry and get a number of quotes before you decide.

Where to get ideas

☐ Look at what other people in your field do and improve on it.
☐ Get help – go to a professional who puts together direct mail packages.
☐ Go to direct mail exhibitions and collect copies of everything.
☐ Get copies of direct mail from other English-speaking countries.
☐ Read magazines and newspapers.

Choose expert help

Shop around and look at several agencies. Ask colleagues and friends. Go to seminars, conferences and trade shows. Approach organisations doing similar work to yours and ask their advice. Ask agencies for a list of clients and talk to them. That is a very valuable source of information.

Finding major donors

Asking for a large donation; overcoming the fear of rejection

The first obstacle faced by anyone asking for a large donation is the fear of rejection. The very thought that someone would think the less of the asker or mock them in any way can paralyse a fundraiser. All of us have listened to a board or fundraising committee decide in principle to ask likely donors for a large contribution, only to stumble when it came to asking the specific person. They say they can't ask their friends for fear of embarrassment. They can't ask their clients for ethical reasons. They can't ask people already donating, it would be too much. Soon there is no one left to ask. 'Pity,' they say, 'it was such a good idea – maybe someone else should ask?' 'Perhaps the fundraiser would be the best,' they conclude. In one neat move the whole opportunity for the board to act effectively and make a major contribution is lost.

The key point for the fundraiser is to be fully aware of the asker's discomfort. Acknowledge openly that asking for money can be a daunting task. Realise that the majority of people are more comfortable asking strangers for money than their friends. Do not take the easy route and say. 'Oh, just start with your friends.' It is an immediate turn-off.

Discuss with your board why they are involved with your organisation. Get them to realise why they feel good about their involvement. Make sure they fully understand the real purpose of your organisation and the needs it fulfils. Show them examples of your work and how it affects real people. Convince them that they should not prejudge other's response. In other words, do not say no for someone else. Tell them to show their commitment to the organisation and let the other person decide to say no for themselves.

Get a list of likely donors

Encourage your board to be practical about the list. Get them to go through their address books and write down the name, address and phone number of anyone who could give a £500 donation.

The best approach

The best approach is to have the person contact the names on their own list. Failing that, they should give their list to another board member, fully brief them and then 'open the door' for them.

Opening the door

'Opening the door' for someone else to ask is much easier than asking yourself. There is no loss of face. This approach can sometimes move you along. The door opener should talk about their involvement with the organisation, explain why the organisation is important – relating this all the time to the interests and concerns of the potential donor. They should finish by saying that they want them to meet a fellow board member, to discuss joining them in becoming a donor. The door opener's case is obviously stronger if they themselves have given a donation – no matter how small.

Remind your board member that homework is vital – offer to do it for them. Know the donor's interests, previous giving patterns, social activities, hobbies. You'll find all of this in *Who's Who*, society pages and business magazines. If the prospective donor agrees to a meeting, then the hardest part of the job is over.

Asking

Do not get stuck at this point. If you've got as far as the meeting you know the person is at least considering giving you a donation. They know why you are meeting them and they haven't said no. It is important to be very well briefed so that you can answer any questions, particularly about the financial affairs of your organisation. Be prepared: having got this far you do not want to fail at the last hurdle.

Legacies

Receiving a letter on your desk telling you that someone has left the organisation £100,000 in their will is the stuff of every fundraiser's dreams. Yet it does happen. The problem is, it does not happen enough.

Fundraising by way of legacies is well worth exploring. For many organisations it is the result of a long relationship which started with small, regular donations. However, while this route is a commendable way of getting legacies it is by no means the only one.

It is possible to build a legacy campaign. Many fundraisers believe that all you have to do is place ads where solicitors will see them and that is your legacy programme launched. Likewise, many not for profit board members think placing ads in the death notice columns of newspapers will encourage people to leave money to their organisation. Despite the fact that both these views fly in the face of reason they are widely held. No one will give you a donation if they do not know you – so why would they give you some of their life savings simply because they saw your ad exhorting them to do so?

What you are struggling with as a fundraiser is people's failure to make wills. It is hard to get money for your organisation from wills if people are not writing wills. Hence the folly of placing ads aimed at the general public.

Legacies – a planned approach

By and large, voluntary organisations treat legacies as a bonus to their fundraising. You'll hear: 'Wonderful if we get income from this source, but let's not count on it.' It is possible to be more proactive than that. The Arthritis Foundation of America has a well-developed legacy programme built up over a number of years at each 'chapter' level. (A 'chapter' is equivalent to our regional or branch structures.)

They adopted the novel approach of offering free advice on making a will. At each local branch they built a volunteer group of people with expertise in the area and offered a free service to members, supporters and donors. The experts were then available for one-to-one consultation. Although people were well aware that it was the Arthritis Foundation that was hosting the seminar, they also believed that it was a genuine initiative to inform and was not a 'secret' sales pitch. In addition, they prepared leaflets, written in plain English, to back up their seminars.

Increasingly, innovative fundraisers are designing their own legacy campaigns. However, there are a number of basic elements you will need.

Table 10.5 Elements of a successful legacy campaign

☐ Prepare a plan.

☐ Recruit a voluntary leader or chairperson to lead the campaign.

☐ Recruit a volunteer panel of relevant experts.

☐ Allocate a budget.

☐ Prepare suitable literature on how to make a will.

☐ Inform everyone associated with your organisation about this new campaign.

☐ Start mentioning it in all your literature.

☐ Print 'Remember us in your will' on all your literature.

☐ Research your target group well.

☐ Research what everyone else is doing – learn.

Where to start

The best advice is to start with your own people. Target existing donors and supporters. As fundraisers we're all guilty of looking to 'the new green field' and ignoring what is under our nose.

A handy tip for identifying your first target group is based on the common-sense observation that older people are more likely to make a will. So, target the older members of your donor base, people who have been donors for a long time. Seek out people in retirement communities, active-aged groups, subscribers to specialist retirement publications. Refine your target group by concentrating on those who are good prospects.

Join other organisations

A number of small voluntary organisations could band together to produce leaflets and set up the seminars or meetings. Join forces with the legal profession – they can often co-sponsor an information campaign.

Involve a celebrity

As with your direct mail campaign involve a celebrity, particularly an older one, as your front person. Use their photograph and make the message come from them.

Summary points

1. All of your fundraising activities must put people first. Develop relation-ships with your 'people'.
2. Do not start up a direct mail campaign until you have fully researched all aspects.
3. Know your AIDA.
4. Build your campaign around an effective message, a well-designed mail package and a well-targeted mailing list.
5. Remember to test and always collect names.
6. Go ahead. Start working on getting major donations. Overcome the biggest inhibitor: the fear of rejection.
7. Don't wait for a legacy to come to you. Adopt a planned approach and build a legacy programme.

11

PARTNERSHIP FUNDRAISING/ SPONSORSHIP: OFFERING SOMETHING IN RETURN

Introduction

Support from the corporate sector, cash donations, sponsorship and other schemes like involving staff in fundraising is increasing.

Pre-tax profits are rising and so there is more money available. Companies are also becoming more aware of the value in getting involved with not for profits in the community. This chapter will help you to capitalise on this trend and to understand the culture they are entering and to know how to make the best case possible.

Some not for profits fear that dealing with the corporate sector will commercialise and diminish their mission and undermine their credibility. Others see the corporate world as another target for raising funds, either by way of donation or sponsorship.

Realistically, it is not possible for any fundraiser to ignore the corporate sector. But on the other hand, it is not like other sources of fundraising in that it requires a special approach, particularly to getting sponsorship. This chapter will help you develop an effective approach.

Corporate giving – what is the reality?

Total cash donations by Charity Aid Foundation's top 500 corporate donors increased by 9 per cent in real terms between 1994–95 and 1995–96. This was the largest increase for some years. CAF found nearly 40 per cent of corporate donors interviewed had raised their level of giving. According to CAF the top donating companies are British Telecom plc, Glaxo, Wellcome plc, National Westminster Bank plc, Marks & Spencer plc and Barclays plc.

The Directory of Social Change estimates a 10 per cent increase in funds from companies from 1994 to 1997. However, despite these big increases British businesses do not give as much as you think. Individual donors still give much more. On average, a company gives less than 0.5 per cent of its pre-tax profits to not for profits.

Focusing on the top 100 corporate donors, as recent research by Corporate Citizen does, shows that the increases seen are due to a handful of organisations and the arrival of some new names in this area.

- ☐ Lottery operator Camelot gave £5 million to its new Camelot Foundation.
- ☐ Lloyds TSB Group gave an extra £3 million to its Foundations.
- ☐ EMI in its centenary year gave £5.7 million to its charity and education programmes.

Profits and not for profits – the great divide

In the past, the relationship between the two groups has been cautious, but hard reality is pushing not for profits towards the commercial world for financial support. The caution was based on the stereotypic image each had of the other – the soft, caring amateur director of the charity vs. the hard-headed, bottom-line manager of a company. These images are outdated. Many not for profits are now run on business lines and the corporate world is learning the value of showing a gentle, caring side in its own community and neighbourhood.

It's a long road

It is easy to focus on the large donation or a big sponsorship deal you read about in the papers and ask: 'Why couldn't we get that?' It is easy to overlook the long hours of research and cultivation that goes before this announcement. In some cases, it could take years to build up to that large commitment.

An excellent approach is to identify a rising star in a company and ask them to get involved in a specific activity. Do not ask them to join your committee in an unfocused way: get them busy on something with an end result. It is crucial that their first involvement results in a success – and within a specific time frame. It is up to you to build on that good experience and draw the person into the organisation. If they are loyal to you they will be an excellent advocate for your organisation and your cause within the corporate world.

How do I get information about companies?

Before approaching any company you must do your basic research. Start locally. Your chances of getting a positive response are far higher from a local company or a bigger company which has a local presence.

Table 11.1 Different types of corporate support

☐ Cash – the most welcome but also the most difficult to get.

☐ Benefit-in-kind – this can take the form of free product and loan of specialist staff (like financial staff to help prepare accounts and budgets)

☐ Gifts of depreciated assets – end of year can see companies offloading products and sometimes this can be a boon to a not for profit.

☐ Sponsorship – Companies can put up quite substantial amounts of money to secure association with a not for profit provided the project fits in with their marketing plans and gives them good exposure.

☐ Allow staff to fundraise for a particular charity.

Decide on a number of potential companies. Create a folder and start keeping everything you find out about each company. Read local papers, business pages of newspapers, business magazines, profiles of senior executives in the press. Keep all the press clippings in your file. Get the company's annual report, marketing and sales materials, in-house magazines and anything else they produce.

Basically you are adopting a detective approach. Observe and collect information on all aspects of the company and its service staff. When you approach the company you will be able to match one of your needs to their interests. You will dramatically improve your chances of getting someone's attention if you know a lot about their products, services, structures and their way of doing business.

There is a new and welcome trend among companies to account for their total community contributions. This is good news as it highlights these novel ways of giving and will encourage more companies, reluctant to give cash, to try this new approach.

Corporate Citizen in recent research highlighted:

In-kind contribution

Camelot made this kind of a contribution, of £700,000, on top of its cash donations.

Staff fundraising

Nat West increased its donations by 30 per cent with more local initiatives involving schools.

Match funding

Barclays made a 19 per cent increase in contributions and has expanded its match funding programme.

Employee volunteering

KPMG has upped the amount of its total contributions by encouraging employee volunteering and the launch of a community brokerage service.

Do not always ask for money

Companies help not for profits in a wide variety of ways. It is important that you know your company before you approach them, thereby allowing you to be imaginative in what you request. All the better if you ask for something that's easy for them to give.

A company giving money and staff: Barclays Bank

Barclays Bank has an employee community programme whereby forty co-ordinators, across Britain, support 140 employee volunteer groups. Each group is given a grant of £1,000 to spend on the charity of its choice. The groups mostly work with children and young people. This scheme has the full support of management with the chairman introducing an annual recognition scheme for individuals and groups of staff's charity work.

Staff as fundraisers: Scope adopted by Ladbrokes

Over the next twelve months staff at Ladbrokes 2,000 shops will take part in fundraising events to support the charity's support teams which provide counselling and practical help to families and individuals affected by cerebral palsy.

Why companies give money to not for profits

The reasons vary. Before you approach a company for money you should try to see inside the mind of corporate executives. You'll increase your chances of success if you understand what motivates them.

For example, approaching companies with a well-known ethical outlook can be useful. The Body Shop's ethical viewpoint is well known and they are donating £500,000 towards the new housing charity Habitat for Humanity Great Britain (HFH GB). Building costs are subsidised by using volunteers to manage and construct houses with donated money and materials.

Table 11.2 Reasons why companies support not for profits

To support education initiatives which will fill gaps
Companies may support education programmes which produce people with particular skills – particularly if those skills are in short supply in the community.

To promote good public relations in the community
Many companies have a policy of donating to organisations which benefit their immediate community. The workforce appreciates this as it affects their families, friends and neighbours.

A social conscience
Some company executives feel that they should give while they are doing well. They feel that if the company announces huge profits it should also announce donations to charity.

A marketing edge
A company may make a business decision and incorporate their gifts into the marketing and PR strategy. Computer companies give products to schools and universities.

It is part of their ethics
Some companies have a particular religious or ethical tradition where philanthropy is a core value. Many of these companies set up trust foundations and endow them each year. We're all aware of the Quaker tradition going back into the nineteenth century.

Programmes supported

The range of programmes supported is exceedingly wide. Corporate donations can be given to scholarships, to found and support chairs in universities, to start new youth programmes and for operating support.

Not surprisingly, companies are cautious about what they support, especially if significant amounts of money are involved. They are very sensitive to bad publicity, because of its adverse affect on sales and shareholders, and so tend to avoid controversial organisations. Companies often support issues that directly affect their customers, like sports companies supporting youth programmes or pharmaceutical or food companies supporting health-related organisations.

Making the approach

The personal approach

Executives are bombarded with proposals every day. Many arrive unsolicited and most end up in the wastepaper bin. Do not fall into that trap. Cut through all the paperwork and get to meet the appropriate executive in

Table 11.3 Reasons companies give for not supporting not for profits

'We do not give to charity'
Our company does not have a tradition of giving, for example: small to medium-sized companies and family-owned and managed companies.

'It's a waste of time'
Company executives view time allocated to not for profits as not strictly related to income-generating work and so a waste of company time.

'Our taxes take care of that'
The belief that the government or private individuals should be supporting the programmes of not for profits. Companies feel they pay taxes and that should be enough.

'Fear of the floodgate'
Companies can receive up to 100 requests for money a week. They are overwhelmed. If they have no structure for processing these requests they can often respond by sending out a standard 'no letter'. Companies can be afraid that if they give a big donation to one charity and it becomes known they will be besieged by other similar organisations.

person. Many people go to enormous lengths to avoid this kind of meeting, often hiding behind glitzy proposal documents. Old hands at this maintain that your chances of success increase by 50 per cent if you have a personal contact.

Table 11.4 Checklist for meeting a company executive

1. Do your research well – know your prospect.
2. What's the company's style – formal or casual?
3. Be confident – Be assertive. No one will give if you're hesitant or unconfident.
4. Listen and observe carefully. Watch and listen twice as much as you talk.
5. Ask lots of questions – this is a great opportunity to learn.
6. Show your belief and passion for your organisation.
7. Do not be defensive if you are quizzed about your organisation.
8. Discuss the programme, but do not mention a figure. Get the person's interest first.
9. Thank the person for the meeting in a follow-up letter.
10. Accept a no with good grace. Learn from the experience.

The formal approach

You may be asked to follow up with a written proposal. The golden rule is: keep it brief. Never go over five pages. Busy executives do not have time to read lengthy proposals. Be concise and make your points clearly. Emphasise the aspects of your proposal of interest to the company. You will know these from your research and from your meeting.

Attach background information, but exercise restraint. Do not send everything the organisation has ever produced. Let others in your organisation or business people on your fundraising committee read the document and comment on it.

When they say no

This is understandably hard to take, especially if you have put a lot of work into your presentation. However, it is vital to view rejection as a stage on your way to successfully getting funding for your programme. Learn from the experience. Call your corporate contact and find out why the funding was refused. Was it the wrong time of year, was it not close enough to the company's interests – what was the problem? If the proposal went before a committee, discover their reasons for rejection. Perhaps they would entertain another approach later in the year.

Sponsorship

Before discussing sponsorship it is crucial to be clear that sponsorship from commercial companies for not for profits is not 'charity giving' or philanthropy. This may seem obvious, but the distinction must be made as it indicates a need for a different approach from the traditional fundraising one, when approaching the corporate world for sponsorship.

Deciding on sponsorship

Your organisation should be clear on its position regarding support from the corporate sector. If it is not, then as a fundraiser you must initiate this discussion and have the position clear before you begin approaching any companies. There is nothing more embarrassing than getting a sponsor for a programme only to discover that half your board have an ethical problem with commercial sponsorship.

To appeal to the marketing department of a large company, a not for profit must see itself in terms of a marketing opportunity for that company. Furthermore, it must see itself as a contributory partner – bringing something positive to the partnership.

Sponsorship is a link between a not for profit and a company, which is put together for a marketing purpose. This link can take a number of forms, from funding a publication bearing their name and logo, to paying for an entire service provided by the not for profit.

What most interests sponsors?

Usually programmes or services which are visible and reach a large number of their customers. This can be seen in Dr Marten's partnership with Shelter. This initiative facilitated the company to approach and influence its target audience – younger consumers – by way of a cause that young people support.

Dr Marten felt that the image of Shelter fitted well with its own brand profile. Sponsorship funded Shelter's four student annual fundraising packs. In addition, a further innovative partnership between Dr Marten, Shelter and the retailer Schuch gave Shelter a percentage of ticket sales from performances at the Edinburgh Festival and a donation from each pair of Dr Marten's sold by Schuch during the event.

Benefit-in-kind gifts

Many companies now see sponsorship of not for profits as being as cost-effective and well-targeted as other marketing tools. They like the mutuality aspect of the relationship. Sponsorship mirrors the emotions of consumers. Sponsorship of an environmental charity or a group working with disadvantaged children will please consumers. It is also well received by employees, politicians and other target groups of importance to the company.

The Samaritans appeared on the European television network MTV. MTV donated £73,000 worth of free air time for a 60–second campaign aimed at young people.

Be proactive

If you decide that sponsorship is for your organisation, be proactive. Do not wait to be approached by companies or their agencies. You will get better results and keep more control if you initiate the contact. Think about it – if a sponsor approaches you they have thought out the commercial angle from their point of view and your negotiating position is correspondingly weaker.

Regions

Large companies like BT have huge sponsorship budgets of over £10 million. Much of this is allocated regionally so not for profits at local level should approach regional offices.

Public relations in the community

Over £350 million is given each year to community relations projects by corporations in the UK. A good example of excellent PR sponsorship can be seen in Nestlé's sponsorship of the Kids Clubs Network educational support programme. They have facilitated the London Mozart Players to team up with Kids Club Network for a national tour to promote music in after school clubs. The musicians will encourage development of music skills.

Cause-related marketing

The phrase cause-related marketing (CRM) is used now in relation to sponsorship. The value of cause-related marketing as a fundraising tool is not fully recognised. Research conducted at the end of 1997 for Business in the Community found that 86 per cent of consumers would buy a product or switch brands if it was associated with a not for profit or cause. This points to a need to explore this area further.

The same survey showed that 70 per cent of marketing directors and 67 per cent of community affairs directors believe CRM will increase in importance over the next few years.

Whom do we approach in the company?

You may think that you should approach the people involved with dispensing funds to charity. On the contrary, the people in the marketing or community affairs departments have more money at their disposal.

Know your organisation's value

Never undersell your organisation. Know your value to the sponsor in terms of your reputation, the value of association with your name and the number of supporters you have.

Count your assets. Do you have a large mailing list, or a membership newsletter or magazine or regional offices and staff? Is your organisation known nationally? Is your name a symbol of excellence? Do you have a famous patron?

When approaching a sponsor have a composite view of all your assets as they relate to that sponsor. Do not go cap in hand. The value of your assets to the sponsor depends on how useful they are in allowing them to reach their target groups or customers.

Some companies are content if their logo is visible on a brochure or video. However, other companies want something more tangible. They want the customer to taste their product, drive their car or get shoppers into their shop.

Be specific in the proposal about the marketing benefits you can offer to the marketing department. Vague generalisations are not enough. Be explicit if you have a promise of radio or television coverage. Show your correspondence with the television or radio company.

The go-between role of the advertising or public relations agency

As a fundraiser you will be approached by agencies representing their clients asking for a meeting to discuss a joint programme. Sometimes you can be asked to submit a proposal on your latest series of special events or new initiatives by a public relations agency for one of their clients.

Forgive me for being suspicious, but I always treat these approaches cautiously. It is best to get to the marketing or public relations person in the sponsorship company reasonably quickly. That person will be more of a decision-maker than the agency person.

The type of approach

You are approaching the marketing department. You are making a sales pitch – you are selling your organisation as a partner of value to them.

Know your organisation's strength – present it as a dynamic organisation which can link their product to a specific segment of the market. Know your organisation's statistics well so you can demonstrate your value.

The marketing department are not interested in your budget deficit or staffing difficulties, only in your value to them.

Many in the business community will have an inaccurate view of the not for profit world. They see it as amateurish and peopled by non-professional do-gooders. So be sensitive to this bad image and project professionalism and competence. Make sure all materials look as professional as possible.

Reporting requirements are different

Reporting on a commercial relationship like this is different from reporting on the use of company money given as a donation. The sponsor will want a hands-on approach and will be more interested in the outcome from their own marketing and PR point of view rather than your service to your clients.

How many potential sponsors do you approach at any one time?

Approach a number of sponsors at once. Do not make the mistake of approaching one company at a time and waiting long periods for a reply. Be prepared to persevere and send your proposals in a number of times.

Sources of information about sponsorship

A number of directories exist, including:

☐ Hollis Sponsorship Yearbook
☐ BRAD
☐ Leading National Advertisers Report
☐ Major Companies Guide from Directory of Social Change.

Summary points

1. Always consider approaching the commercial sector for support – either financial or benefit-in-kind.
2. Before approaching any company do your background research well.
3. Be aware of why companies support not for profits and use it to tailor your approach to each company.
4. Prepare well before making your initial approach by using the checklist provided.
5. Sponsorship is not philanthropy. Companies use sponsorship for marketing and public relations so tailor your approach accordingly.
6. Be proactive about sponsorship.

12

ORGANISING THE UNUSUAL: MOTIF CAMPAIGNS AND EMERGENCY APPEALS

Introduction

This chapter will help you if you are thinking about running a major motif campaign or an emergency appeal. Both types of fundraising require careful planning and meticulous attention to detail.

This chapter will help you with your choice of motif. The components of a sample plan are outlined to give you the basics for planning your own campaign.

Emergency appeals can overwhelm a fundraiser or fundraising department so it is important to anticipate what is required and to pre-plan as much as possible. The crucial elements of this approach are outlined.

Motif campaigns: ingredients for success

An attractive way to fundraise is to choose a motif or gimmick and to sell this to the public for a small sum – usually a pound. The best known are Red Nose Day and Daffodil Day. There are many others.

It must be remembered that the prime purpose is to raise money, so pay careful attention to the costings and the bottom line. Don't get involved in something which is exclusively PR-driven – this should be primarily a fundraising exercise.

In addition to good financial control, the other ingredients for success are a good product, a good network of sellers, good logistics to ensure timely and efficient distribution, good public relations and good planning.

Choice of motif

In choosing your motif you must think about what will interest people.

Table 12.1 Choosing a motif

☐ What is the unit cost of the motif?

☐ How much can I afford to pay per unit?

☐ Do I have a unit cost for all additional activities, like PR, distribution, printing?

☐ Is my source of supply reliable?

☐ Have I checked out a number of suppliers?

☐ Will it be ready in sufficient numbers? What guarantees do I have?

☐ Do I have a long enough lead-in time?

☐ Can I service it locally or will high costs mean I have to source it abroad?

☐ Have I market-tested a sample (even among volunteers and friends)?

☐ Has anyone used this motif before?

☐ Will it be easy to build a PR campaign around this motif?

☐ Can I ensure reliable quality control over large numbers?

Choose something that will catch their eye. Other factors to consider are listed in Table 12.1.

A useful start is to hold a brainstorming meeting with some creative people. Include some sales and marketing people to get input on that aspect and also include public relations input. Most importantly, involve your volunteers and potential sellers – they have a keen sense of what will work on the ground.

Do research on all the other motif campaigns that have been run – learn from them. Some of them are extremely high-profile like Red Nose Day and are backed up by massive TV coverage. You might want to look at others that do it without TV coverage.

Build your volunteer network

If you are contemplating a regional or nationwide motif campaign think long and hard about whether you have the volunteer resources to sell the motif. Common sense will tell you that even if you have an attractive motif backed up by good PR, you won't make any money if people can't buy it.

During the six years that I ran the Arthritis Foundation of Ireland's Butterfly Campaign a recurrent constraint was getting volunteers to sell the butterfly. Many not for profits running this kind of campaign have had the same experience. If you have a good network of branches, service centres or clients, you are halfway there. If you are a centralised organisation with little field backup you should give the idea serious thought before starting.

A campaign plan for a national fundraising appeal

To organise a national fundraising appeal you must have a campaign plan.

1. Get an overview of your targets and their geography

First, define the area you intend to target. A useful rule to follow is to get a copy of the census and make it your 'new best friend'. Using the census you should study the demographics on a national or regional basis to familiarise yourself with your potential market. You can then work out the maximum number of people you can target.

You now begin to prioritise and assemble your target groups, recognising that you cannot possibly target the whole population.

Second, you must decide the geographical areas you intend to target. Divide the population into smaller groups, cities, towns, rural districts, neighbourhoods, whichever is most appropriate. They can be chosen for any number of reasons, e.g., you could have a good branch structure or good regional workers, or it could be the location of one of your service centres.

2. Now get a map and have a look at the location of your target groups

Consult the census and subdivide the area into different population centres, cities, towns, etc. You could decide to focus on one major city. In that instance, subdivide the city into districts. The key point is to know your total target population and to subdivide it into manageable units.

Now that you are clear on the total number of people you are targeting and their location you should draw up a chart showing the priority for action. To illustrate this let's think about planning a fundraising campaign in a densely urbanised county. In this instance the towns are crucial, so list them with their populations. Start with the highest population and work down, that way you can prioritise the areas of greater potential return. If you run out of time you will only miss out the smaller ones. You now have your total target split into sub-units based on relative size.

3. Get volunteers

Now you have to find volunteers to help you fundraise in each town. You have turned your mammoth task into a series of smaller tasks. This is a far easier task than fundraising a whole country or trying to do it yourself.

There is never a good time to get volunteers to do anything, but particularly when you ask people to fundraise. Aunts, cousins, friends all develop mystery illnesses – children have amazingly complicated homework and projects. But relax, getting volunteers to fundraise is not easy but it is possible.

Organising a large-scale motif campaign involves a huge variety of different tasks. This allows you to approach volunteers separately to help you with quite specific tasks. You will find asking someone to do a specific job is the most effective way of getting a volunteer. Be clear, be specific, be convincing and be realistic about the amount of time you require from them. In short, be organised and professional.

Remember you are asking someone to do a specific task within a specific time. They will say yes or no – accept both with equal grace. Never, never pressurise anyone. It always backfires. You must build your campaign out of a mosaic of tiny pieces – each place, each person, each task. If you don't ask too much of one person then they won't let you down, but even if they do, the overall mosaic will stay in place and you can quickly plug the gap.

A time chart must be prepared setting the start and finish dates for the fundraising project.

If you want to involve someone in a fundraising event you must be fully committed to what you are doing and you must answer with certainty a number of key questions. They provide clarity of purpose for prospective volunteers.

1. Can I explain in one sentence what I am fundraising for?
2. Do I believe in the activity/project for which I am fundraising?
3. What is my target?
4. How many people live in the area where I intend to fundraise?

In writing a fundraising plan *believe in what you are doing*. You cannot convince other people, especially reluctant people, to fundraise unless you first convince them that your efforts are for something worthwhile. You may not realise it, but they know how valuable their time is.

4. Distribute effectively

When organising a motif campaign one of the most physically demanding aspects can be getting your motif, containers, publicity material out to all your volunteers.

You can always hive it off to a distribution company but the costs can be alarming and may make the whole project unviable.

Using volunteers to pack and load, and distributing the materials yourself, can reduce costs, but it does tend to wear out staff and volunteers. I did this when organising a campaign – but only in year one. We learnt our lesson about not exhausting your volunteers after that.

Our solution was to get a major international delivery company to sponsor distribution by way of a benefit-in-kind gift. They distributed our motifs around the country free of charge. We did all the paperwork, in triplicate, to reduce the burden on their staff. It provided an excellent PR opportunity with photographs of their staff and vehicles appearing in national and trade press. The partnership was so good they stayed associated for five years.

5. Work hard to get good public relations

Good public relations is the motor of any motif campaign. You are essentially persuading people to contribute to your organisation's work while giving them something small, but tangible, in return.

In your public relations you are creating an awareness of the whole campaign and secondly of the organisation. People are reacting to the motif, so you build a story, a set of images, a magic around it.

You want people to look for the motif, or at least recognise what it is when they see it. As any salesperson will tell you, it is very difficult if you have to educate the person before you make your sales pitch. And it is quite impossible to do all of that in a few seconds as the person walks past. If you use your PR to create awareness, then each encounter is a straight sales one.

These motif campaigns are only worthwhile if they run over a number of years and momentum is allowed to build up. Your first year can be the most difficult, but second time around you will have ironed out most the creases. For example, you'll know how to make your motif interesting for press photographers.

6. Allow enough time

This brings you to another dimension and that is timing. Giving yourself enough time to organise the campaign is fundamental to your success.

A time chart must be prepared setting the start and finish dates for the fundraising project.

Remember the product cycle

Motif campaigns, like any other product, are subject to the phenomenon known as the product cycle. They start slowly, build up, peak, plateau and then begin to decline. This concept is explained in detail in chapter 3. The trick is to know where your motif campaign is on the cycle and to have your next fundraising initiative ready to roll, as your motif campaign begins to decline.

As a fundraiser this can be a hard to face. You've built up a very successful campaign and it is building and building. It is discouraging to start thinking about a replacement in the midst of success.

Smart fundraisers are always thinking of the next campaign. Sometimes it is hard to bring a fundraising committee around to this point of view.

Keeping careful records of sales at all levels and comparing performance year on year will give you an early indication of where you are in the cycle.

Emergency appeals

Many organisations become involved in some form of emergency work, no matter what field they are in. However, one type of organisation which deals constantly with unforeseen and major emergencies is a third world aid organisation. Floods, earthquakes or sudden movements of refugees happen unexpectedly and can catch organisations unprepared.

I have worked in two large organisations which have run major emergency programmes and the principal lesson that I learnt was that, no matter how unexpected an event or how seriously it taxes your resources, you cannot succeed without a plan – in effect, if you don't take charge of the situation it will quickly take charge of you.

In dealing with an unexpected event which looks like it is going to take over all your other fundraising or PR work you must decide quickly what major tasks have to be accomplished – who is going to be responsible and by when you want them to be completed.

Planning – even in an emergency

Being in control and having an overview are basic requirements. You cannot do everything yourself, so you must delegate but with knowledge and according to a plan so that all your objectives are met.

Bring your people around you and quickly make a list of all the jobs you can think of. Be flexible, as other things may well crop up. You are anticipating the broadest range of problems by doing this. Try to anticipate all the tasks imaginable.

An instance when I've had to do this was when the Irish Red Cross Society launched a major appeal for Romania in the early 1990s. Romania was in chaos; President Ceauşescu and his wife had been shot. The International Committee of the Red Cross had requested air-lifted medical and other emergency supplies. It was Christmas and everyone was on holiday and it seemed that everything but the Irish Red Cross Society was closed.

We held an emergency meeting of staff and made a list of all the tasks as we initially saw them. We later had to add to the list as we had underestimated the need for people to answer phones and take credit card donations. Once we made an overall plan we assigned tasks to everyone and let them start work.

In no time we were getting results and the pieces of the puzzle began to connect. We got planes from an Irish airline, Ryanair, which had a strong

Romanian connection. We got managing directors of pharmaceutical companies and suppliers to open for us, even though it was Christmas.

The key lesson is to anticipate what you need and to think through your response. This chapter highlights areas where you need to pre-plan so that you will be able to deal with the fundraising or PR in any emergency situation.

Getting the financial resources

The first thing to realise is that in an emergency funds will come from a variety of sources. You need to be working on all of these at the same time.

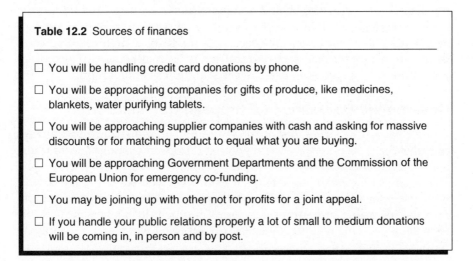

Table 12.2 Sources of finances

☐ You will be handling credit card donations by phone.

☐ You will be approaching companies for gifts of produce, like medicines, blankets, water purifying tablets.

☐ You will be approaching supplier companies with cash and asking for massive discounts or for matching product to equal what you are buying.

☐ You will be approaching Government Departments and the Commission of the European Union for emergency co-funding.

☐ You may be joining up with other not for profits for a joint appeal.

☐ If you handle your public relations properly a lot of small to medium donations will be coming in, in person and by post.

Handling a rush of small donations

When an emergency appeal is launched a flood of small donations will follow. It is vital that you put in place the procedures to record them and to issue receipts. You must record names and addresses, as they are vital for your database for future direct mail.

There is nothing different in this from your normal procedures, other than the sheer volume. Keep your procedures simple. You may need to use volunteers, so write your procedures down and have these instructions ready to give out. The accounts department will handle all the details, but as the fundraiser it is important that you explain what you may be unleashing. This is particularly true of a not for profit launching its first major appeal.

Credit card donations

As a fundraiser you will want to make it as easy as possible for people to give you money. You must ensure that you have registered with the credit card companies and banks as a merchant so that you can process donations made using credit cards. You will need to have extra phone lines and the people to man them. These people will need clear instructions on how to fill in forms. Make sure you have large supplies of forms.

Gifts of product

When you are responding to a major emergency you will need to purchase large volumes of supplies. You will be spending a lot so you have some leverage. When dealing with companies, negotiate discounts for cash purchases or the donation of additional products.

My experience is that companies are very amenable to this type of negotiation. They may welcome receiving publicity in return. Some companies are happy for their senior executives to be associated with the not for profit and to be included in press releases and press photographs.

Government Departments/European Commission

When raising large amounts of money under pressure you must always consider the possibility of government or European Commission funding. Some preparatory networking with key people is possible and useful.

In a quiet time before an emergency hits you, you should make contact with the relevant officials and meet them. Get all necessary background material regarding procedures and forms and be fully conversant with the arrangements. This will greatly speed up approval when you are applying for funding in a crisis.

Contact representative lobbying bodies for Non-Governmental Organisations in Brussels and also the relevant officials in the Commission. There are information days and training courses which are well worthwhile attending. These funders want to make it easier for you and it is in their interests that you are familiar with all the procedures.

Joint appeals

If you are contemplating working with other not for profits in a joint appeal it makes very good sense to have made contact with your fundraising equivalents and to have established a working relationship.

Fundraising volunteers

When an emergency occurs the fundraiser is affected in two ways: funds are needed urgently and donations start pouring in. For any fundraiser this is going to create resource problems. So if you work in an organisation where this kind of situation is likely to arise once a year or more you need to give some serious thought to building an emergency task force.

Choose level-headed people who won't panic. Draw up a plan of what tasks need to be carried out and assign a number of volunteers to them. Meet your volunteers and brief them on the task. Take your time and build up a corps of volunteers ready to come to your assistance at short notice. They must be able to work long or odd hours for a short, intensive period.

Write down your procedures and keep them in a folder. Put the names and contact numbers for all your volunteers into it. Time spent on this will repay you handsomely when an emergency overtakes you.

Public relations aspect of an emergency

Public relations are an integral part of a not for profit's response to an emergency. There is a progression from informing people about what is happening though to reporting on what the not for profit has done. The stages are set out in Table 12.3.

Public relations are needed to create an awareness of the problem and to galvanise support for the organisation's work.

Issue press releases and share information with the media. Invite journalists to visit your offices to report on, or film, your response. Prepare specialised briefings for key journalists, if appropriate. If you are working with other funders liaise with their public relations personnel to avoid unnecessary duplication.

The fundraisers may see a fall in response after a day or so, especially if the emergency drops out of the news, and may require the public relations people to regenerate interest.

Table 12.3 Public relations aspects of emergency appeals

☐ Initial information about the emergency

☐ Your organisation's response

☐ Needs of people and what your organisation needs to respond to

☐ Publicise fundraising targets if appropriate

☐ Provide continuous updates on the emergency situation

☐ Give periodic reports on your organisation's actions

☐ Give a full and final report on the benefits of your organisation's activities in the emergency

☐ Generously thank everyone who helped

To be really effective in publicising an emergency and to co-ordinate both PR and fundraising activity, it is vital that you brief yourself very well at the beginning. It is also vital that you stay on top of the unfolding situation.

At the beginning there is a temptation to issue an immediate statement. My advice is: take an hour to read all the background materials – it will pay off later when you are under pressure. You'll be on certain ground.

Designate spokespeople and ensure that they are well briefed to speak on the subject. Have a number of spokespeople who can handle different aspects, like the medical or technical as well as the not for profit angle. This is most important when faced with regenerating media interest. You need to come up with a fresh angle. Fieldworkers describing the problems and what the money raised is doing to help will often get you renewed interest.

Summary points

Motif campaign

1. Choose your motif very carefully with an eye to its costs and appeal. Use the checklist to help you choose.
2. Adapt the sample plan for a national campaign to suit your particular circumstances.
3. Always use the census and relevant maps to establish your target groups.
4. Build a good volunteer and distribution network.
5. Always remember to watch for your position on the product cycle.

Emergency appeals

1. Planning is crucial to any emergency appeal.
2. It is useful to pre-plan and set up procedures which can be used for the initial stages of an emergency appeal – this refers especially to the procedures for handling a large influx of small cash or credit card donations.
3. Build up a corps of volunteers who will respond to an urgent response for help.
4. Make strategic use of public relations throughout the emergency appeal.

13

YOUR BREAD AND BUTTER: SMALL-SCALE OR LOCAL FUNDRAISING

Introduction

This chapter will help you if you are starting out in fundraising, particularly in a small to medium-sized organisation. It outlines some pointers to get you started, including how to fundraise from the grassroots.

Starting fundraising in a newly established organisation

Start fundraising at once

If you are setting up an organisation or a lobbying campaign start raising your funds at the earliest possible chance. Make sure people realise that whatever the cause is, you will need money. Someone has to pay for the hall you are meeting in and for the posters and placards. It may not be much, but you do need funds.

Involve the people you serve in your fundraising

Since it is usually the community that needs your organisation's services, good fundraising means going out to that community and letting them know what you are doing. Give them the opportunity to get involved, to contribute. Let the community own your work – you exist to service their needs so let them feel involved enough to contribute to your work.

People give to people

Always focus on the fact that you are raising money for *people*. Don't try to enthuse people by talking about financial deficits, meeting staff costs or other operational terms. The saying 'people give to people' has been tried and tested and found to be true. Sell the way you are reaching people and changing their lives for the better. Talk about the loss to people if you close due to lack of funds.

Plan to have fun

All fundraising involves people one way or another, so when planning your fundraising always keep this human element in mind. People like to enjoy themselves even while working for a good cause. Plan fun into all stages from the initial planning through the sales drive and into the evaluation.

Have a celebration meal, tell jokes, lighten up. If you get the reputation of being very serious or tetchy under pressure, then although people may work with you on the current campaign they won't come back again.

Avoid crisis fundraising: plan for one year's operating budget

Crisis fundraising does not send the right signal to potential donors, especially if they see you lurch from one deficit to another. Your donors will begin to doubt your ability to manage and plan, and your volunteers' confidence will be badly shaken. They will begin to ask if the organisation is really meeting a need if no one is prepared to support the organisation financially.

It is good practice when setting up to ensure that you have a year's operational budget in the bank at all times. Then, if the worst happens and a number of fundraising projects fail, you will still have time to regroup and launch new fundraising initiatives.

Living on the financial edge has become a way of life in many not for profits. It can be habit-forming. Some organisations regard it as a badge of honour – they are so busy working that they have no time to worry about fundraising. This is difficult for the fundraiser, because fundraising is not given a chance. You appear rather shaky to your donors and look like a poor investment.

Is hiring a fundraiser the solution to our fundraising problems?

The answer is an emphatic NO. No one fundraiser, no matter who they are or what skills they have, can raise the total budget single-handed. They can try, but they will burn out very fast. A good fundraiser will work *with* the board, staff and volunteers, steering them through a planned fundraising programme.

Many chairpeople or directors, when faced with a looming deficit, advertise and hire a fundraiser. They set them up in an office and leave them to their own devices, having first set them a notional fundraising target.

They and the board members are often surprised when the fundraiser leaves after six months. They didn't realise that they have set up an impossible situation.

What do fundraising consultants do?

Really good fundraising consultants do not raise money themselves. They do something much more valuable. They enable the organisation to find the best way to raise money. Remember the old adage: 'Give me a fish and I'm fed for a day, but teach me to fish and I'll feed myself.'

Fundraising consultants can be enormously helpful if they work with the board defining its role and its fundraising plans. But ultimately the hard work must be done by the organisation itself.

By all means hire consultants with specialist skills to help you with different fundraising projects like direct mail, running large-scale events, lotteries or covenant campaigns, but don't imagine that a fundraising consultant will raise all your funds for you.

One last word about hiring fundraising consultants. Always check their references, not only to verify their bona fides, but also to ensure that they have the necessary skills for your needs.

Fundraising from your own grassroots

This type of fundraising focuses on getting money from people who need and want your organisation and its services. You go to ordinary people who are committed to your organisation. When you raise money from this level of giver you prove that there are a lot of people who support your organisation and that people want your services.

This is an excellent jumping-off point when you are approaching large companies or foundations. They know you are not going to become dependent on them for grants as you have baseline support in your own community. They are reassured that if they support a particular programme for three years you will be able to meet your running costs from your own resources.

An additional benefit is that grassroots fundraising lets you know which programmes the community really values. If people donate to your campaign for a drop-in centre, but resist your efforts to open a library, it might be time to reconsider your priorities.

The pound-by-pound approach to fundraising

As a fundraiser you have to be wary of the volunteers and fundraising committees who want to reduce fundraising targets to getting individual pounds from separate donors. They decide they want to raise £20,000 and want to ask 1,000 people to donate £20 each. This is frustrating for a fundraiser because it uses up so much time, is difficult to run and wears people out for very little return.

Membership drive

A membership drive is when you ask people to join your organisation for a small fee. This entitles them to priority access to your services. You are asking a highly targeted group of people to contribute and you are telling them about the benefits of your programmes to them. If you serve your members well and focus on meeting their real needs, they will remain loyal to your organisation.

Advantages of a membership programme

For some not for profits offering membership has a number of advantages.

☐ Membership builds loyalty and allows people feel a sense of ownership of the organisation.

☐ Membership builds a deeper commitment. People feel they are more important than a mere source of money.

☐ Membership conditions people to renew their donation each year, because they feel more committed to the organisation.

Membership programmes tend to result in more generous donors. People who join as a member, unlike one-off donors, usually stay with the organisation longer and give larger donations.

This type of fundraising results in a steady and reliable income which funds your basic running costs. It is particularly suitable for community-based organisations or specific issues, like health charities.

Summary points

1. If you are setting up a not for profit from scratch it is never too early to fundraise.
2. Remember that people give to people.
3. Look first to your grassroots for support.
4. Consider the merits of a membership drive.

14

ASKING BIG BROTHER: GRANTS

Introduction

Increasingly, not for profits are looking to grant-giving bodies for financial support. In fact, giving money away is now big business. There is no one way to apply for a grant, particularly as each grant-giving body has its own criteria. However, there are certain elements which will improve the professionalism of your application. This chapter will equip you with the essentials.

Giving money away is big business

There are over 3,000 registered charities which exist to give grants to other organisations. They have an annual budget of over £1 billion.

There is a huge variation in these trusts from the largest – the Wellcome Trust with a grant-giving capacity of £218 million in 1997 – to the smallest, which dispense less than £1 million per annum. The top five grant-making trusts and their annual grants for 1997 were:

Wellcome Trust – £218 million.
National Lottery – £158 million.
British Academy – £22 million.
Royal Society – £21 million.
Garfield Weston Foundation – £19 million.

All of the charitable grant-giving trusts are governed by charity law. In practice most trusts prefer to give to other not for profit organisations rather than to individuals.

Finding the right source of funds

Before you begin writing, spend some time identifying the right funding source. This is a crucial stage in applying for a grant. Most Foundations and Government bodies state the type of activity they will support. Don't waste your resources by applying to the wrong source.

A number of publications list sources of money. The best known are published by Charities Aid Foundation and The Directory of Social Change.

What are Foundations?

Foundations are organisations set up to give money away. Some are set up by an individual or family in order to take a more organised approach to giving money to individuals and not for profits. Others are established by companies to manage the many requests they receive for help. Levels of staffing in Foundations vary, as do their application procedures.

What is a grant proposal?

It is a written document submitted to a grant-making body requesting funds for an organisation or a specific programme.

There are as many grant proposal forms as there are grant-making bodies. So be prepared to write a different one each time.

Writing proposals for grants is highly competitive, but there is a good deal of help available – including books from some of the organisations listed in the Appendix.

Writing the application

There is a considerable amount of mystery surrounding writing grant applications. A good deal too much mystery! Every foundation has a slightly different approach. The key to success is to read the application carefully and follow the guidelines. If they ask for a particular piece of information, give it to them. You don't want your application to be rejected simply because you failed to provide the right information. The demand for funds outweighs the supply – so an incorrect application will fall at the first hurdle.

Keep up to date on new rounds of grants

It is important to be aware of time scales for grant applications. Different rounds of grant-giving are announced throughout the year and many have closing dates. Read the specialist charity magazines such as *Charity* published by Charities Aid Foundation (CAF). For example, in January 1998:

☐ The Heritage Lottery Fund announced £11.5 million worth of grants as part of its ongoing urban parts programme.
☐ The Earthwatch Millennium Award Scheme announced its 1998 application round for awards. About £1.4 million was made available for overseas study.

Table 14.1 Checklist for grant applications

DO'S	DON'T'S
Keep it simple and direct. Use short words and sentences. Avoid jargon known only to your field of work.	Don't be vague and unclear in your objectives.
Open with a compelling statement of your need.	Don't make the funders guess what you are trying to achieve – they won't. They'll simply pass on to the next application.
Define the problem and the solution – stress the urgency of the need.	Don't be unclear about the results you want to achieve. Funders are giving you money – they want to know what to expect in return.
Be clear about your plan of implementation.	Don't be technical in your writing style. Don't use jargon.
Clear controlled budget Funders dissect budgets for padding and lack of control. Do your research well and make your costs realistic. Include everything.	Don't be unrealistic in your budget – avoid asking for too much or to little.
Bolster your credibility Show your successes. Prove you can carry this project out because you have an excellent track record. Include these in your proposal. Mention awards or special recognitions you have received. Include press cuttings.	Don't be overconfident that your programme is wonderful. Ensure that you clearly show that your plan will solve the problem you stated. Prove you have the experience, qualified people and management experience to carry this out.
Show lasting benefits Grant-givers like to see things with a lasting benefit. They don't like to see their money filling a gap in your funding difficulties. They will respond positively to clearly stated and backed-up benefits.	Don't rely on one funder for the whole budget. You can build a large mosaic up with support from a number of sources. However, be completely transparent about donors and funders.
Give your application a dry run Give your proposal to colleagues or friends outside your organisation. Ask them to ask hard questions. You'll learn a lot from their comments.	

☐ The Johnson & Johnson European Fund for Children's Health was launched with a closing date in mid-February.

Fundamentals of writing the proposal

Tailor the proposal to suit the funds

Research the organisation you are approaching very carefully. Be clear about their funding preferences. Consult the many directories of Trusts and Foundations and find those that most closely suit the programme for which you are seeking funds.

Clarity of purpose

Before you begin writing a grant application it is essential that you clarify the purpose of the programme. Consult widely with staff, board members, volunteers, clients and beneficiaries. If the idea is half-baked this will affect the proposal. Thrash out the objectives, target groups, results – everything.

In addition to clarity it is important that your programme fits within the overall mission and goals of the organisation. No funds will touch a proposal that does not dovetail with the rest of the organisation's activities.

Establish your credibility

You must establish your organisation's credibility. You must show that you understand the problem and are aware of what others may already be doing to tackle it. No one organisation has the answer.

Prove your credentials for tackling the problem. Highlight the experience of key staff and board members, refer to publications, membership of taskforces or expert committees. You may know you are excellent in your field, but you still have to demonstrate it. Show your management capabilities.

Make your proposal real to people

There is a temptation to resort to jargon when faced with guidelines and forms. You are comfortable with it and it explains everything succinctly, doesn't it? No, it does not. Nothing puts people off more than the inside language of certain sectors of the voluntary sector. Try to see it from the Foundation's point of view. What does this sentence mean: 'The NGOs in third world development feel that ODA as a percentage of GNP should be increased to reach the DAC-OECD average'?

You should concentrate on making the needs of your organisation real in terms of the people you wish to help. Always remember people give to people – even in Foundations it is a person who makes the decision. Show the problem and benefits in terms of people.

A not for profit applying for funds for a horticultural project for disabled teenagers described their work in the following terms: 'Teaching 500 young people how to turn seeds into flowers and helping these teenagers to plant seeds of self-worth and hope in their own future.' They could have spoken about serving young adults with a horticultural project.

Beware becoming reliant on grants

Foundations are reluctant to fund administrative expenses; they prefer to fund separate programmes or projects. But there is a danger in setting up programmes in the knowledge that funding will be available. When funding runs out the programme can lapse leaving the beneficiaries high and dry. There is then a temptation to set up another programme to get new funds.

If this happens, the original mission of the organisation may be over- looked. Many a voluntary organisation, particularly smaller ones, loses its way when funding is difficult and they start to chase the pounds.

It is essential to have a core of donors and supporters and to supplement this base with grants. If you become dependent on one or more grants for your survival, you have put all your 'funding eggs' in one basket – that's never a good idea.

Evaluation – the keyword

If there is one word which reassures grant-givers it is evaluation. They like to know that you have thought the whole project through to the results stage and that you intend to evaluate it.

It reassures them that you can foresee the planned results and they can evaluate progress against the stated results. These results must be quanti- fied. It is no use saying 'we will meet the need' or 'we will give help to many old people'. It is impossible to evaluate something as woolly as that. It must be something like '500 young people will receive training in our early school leavers programme over two years.'

Community foundations

This is a North American idea. Community foundations have existed there for most of the twentieth century. In Britain they began about ten years ago and are still quite rare. These Foundations create locally based trusts which endeavour to get 'new' money from businesses and individuals in particular local areas. They aim to build up a large endowment fund which will make funds available for some considerable time. Opinions vary, but something over £2 million is needed to give the trust a fighting chance.

These are new and exciting ideas so find out about them and, if you can, get involved. The Association of Community Trusts & Foundations (ACTAF) will help you.

Summary points

1. Do your research and match your application to the funding orientation of the grant-giving body.
2. Follow the checklist outlining the major Do's and Don'ts.
3. Follow the funders guidelines carefully and give them all the information they require, in the format they specify.
4. Make your proposal real to people.
5. Be careful not to become overreliant on grants or on any one funding agency.

Part 3

GET DOWN TO IT –
YOUR PLANS AND
YOUR PR KIT

Introduction

The third and final part of the book builds on the earlier parts by helping you to apply what you have discovered in a very practical way. In chapter 15 you will find your basic PR tools and in chapter 16 you can copy and use the various charts to write your own plan.

15

GET YOUR BASIC PR TOOLS READY

Introduction

Throughout this book the link between PR and fundraising has been made. In this chapter you will find the information you need to help you achieve this in concrete terms.

Advice on how to prepare your three basic PR tools – your press contact list, press releases and press pack – is given. This is followed by hints on how to make the most of these tools. Events are a crucial part of PR, and so you'll find the comprehensive checklist for an event very useful. The practical advice on staging press conferences and other events will help you greatly. Finally, you'll find some hints on organising a protest.

Target your public relations

Public relations, like fundraising, should be approached in a planned way. The public should be divided into separate target groups, called 'publics' in PR terms, to whom highly specific messages are sent. Your public relations 'publics' should be chosen with the input of all in the fundraising department. A third world charity, lobbying for changes in international trade arrangements, will send a highly detailed statistical message to parliamentarians, but focus on the plight of individuals in their message to regular donors.

The role of public relations in fundraising

The not for profit world is a constantly changing one. 1997 saw big changes with a renewal of government commitment to its key role in the economy. Not for profits are increasingly conscious of what people think of them. Why? First, demands on not for profits are increasing and they are looking to what their constituents or client group think of them. Are they meeting the real needs? Are they delivering an efficient service? Do they listen to their beneficiaries?

Second, resources are not keeping pace with the increasing demands. Not for profits are working harder to raise the same amount of money. Fundraising is now run on commercial lines. Competition is strong and fundraisers must be very conscious of serving their donor. The role of donors and their view of the organisation are crucial.

Public relations plays a key role in shaping clients' and donors' views of your not for profit. As with fundraising, an overall plan is needed. It is usual to plan the year in advance and to combine public relations and fundraising activities.

Public relations

Good public relations is a two-way communication between you and others built on increasing understanding. You define the different groups or 'publics' you want to communicate with and tailor a specific message to them. You can communicate with a range of different groups at the same time. For example, in fundraising you can be telling the media about an award your education programme has won while simultaneously lobbying your local authority for more money. You may also be communicating the success of your programme with your major donors so that they will know how their money is being spent.

Without public relations the fundraiser is operating in a vacuum. You can't ask people to contribute to an organisation they know nothing about. Even if people have heard of you, they may be confusing you with a similar organisation or they may have heard bad reports. Remember that there is no such thing as no public relations – people will form an impression of your organisation even if you carry out no PR activities. It's far better if you can shape their view rather than let them do it themselves.

Public relations – a professional approach

Public relations is so important to your fundraising success that it must be done professionally. Fundraising and public relations must be linked. Don't fall into the trap of running a fundraising event and excusing its poor financial return by saying it was good for PR. Fundraising and public relations may be linked but they are not interchangeable. You should run both your fundraising and public relations with good strategic plans and with an eye to results. There are a number of common management practices you'll recognise in Table 15.1.

Management by good idea (MBGI) in fundraising is a lot more common than you might think. This is when the fundraising and PR people lurch from event to event because it seemed like a good idea at the time.

Table 15.1 Common management practices

MBO	Management by objectives.
MBWA	Management by walking around and collecting ideas.
MBGI	Management by good idea.

A written annual PR plan

Your public relations activities must be set out in a written plan with explicit objectives and deadlines. All of the points in chapters 3 and 4 on planning will be relevant here.

Three basic PR tools

There are a number of tools which every fundraiser needs. They are:

1. Press contact list
2. Press release
3. Press pack

Press contact list

This is the PR person's most important tool. If you're starting off in PR it deserves a lot of time and effort to set it up. You should be systematic about establishing who the major press contacts are in your particular area. You can use a card index file or put your names into one of the special contact manager software programs now available. I recommend both.

Have a separate card for each contact and file them by category. You will build your own system, but some of the basic categories are listed in Table 15.3. Record everyone's name, address, phone, fax and e-mail numbers. Update your list regularly.

Building relationships with journalists

Remember that journalists are people too. Go beyond keeping lists and build a good relationship with them. Phone them up, meet them. Tell them what you are planning. Ask them for advice and help. If you succeed in

Table 15.2 PR plan in support of fundraising

Analysis of Present Situation
What is your mission? What are your most important programmes? What challenges do you face in fundraising or volunteer recruitment? Who is your competition? What are they doing?

Objectives
If your public relations programme could only accomplish seven things for the organisation this year, what would they be?

Target Audiences
Who do you need to reach for your organisation's fundraising to succeed? Who are the potential donors you need to reach to prepare the way for a fundraising campaign?

Key Messages
Are the messages you choose to communicate through your public relations consistent with your other messages, e.g., your programmes? Have you crafted specific messages for each of your specific audiences?

Target Media
How do you reach your publics with your message? What media most influence them?

Strategies
What specific communications strategies will help your organisation meet its volunteer recruitment and fundraising objectives?

Specific Activities
What are the twenty specific activities you will undertake this year? The more specific you are, the easier it is to measure your progress each month. Make sure the activities aren't just every good idea you have, but rather the means to achieve your stated objectives.

Staffing
What staff, volunteer resources or outside consultants will it require to carry out the specific activities?

Finances
You need financial resources to accomplish your plan. Spell them out clearly in the plan – and if there's pressure to cut the budget, start by determining which objectives or specific activities your organisation does not want to accomplish.

Seasonal Fluctuations
Does your organisation serve more people during the summer? Is year-end your busiest fundraising time? Incorporate the key seasonal factors of your organisation onto your plan and be certain to time PR activities to support them. Are you part of a national organisation with umbrella programmes you can tie into? What outside events are there in the coming year that you should tie into? Election? Back to school? Put these on your calendar to track how everything ties together – and be sure you're not missing opportunities.

Evaluation

You need specific measurements agreed by you and the rest of the management team for the PR plan. Remember, they shouldn't be FR goals (that's for the fundraisers), but instead they should be tied to your specific objectives of supporting fundraising, and other programmes.

Table 15.3 Sample press contact list for a health charity

National papers

Editor

Photo editor

Features editor

Medical or health editor or correspondent

Any columnist taking an interest in health.

Regional papers

Editor

Health magazines and specialist medical publications

Editor

Journals or newsletters of professionals in health care area

National Radio and TV ; consult *TV Times*

Local radio stations; build up names of presenters

---

developing a relationship when you need coverage you'll have an ally not just a name.

The effective press release

A press release is a short document – one to two pages at most – which lets the media know what you are announcing. It is a cheap and effective way of communicating with them, provided it is done in a format the media find useful. Its effectiveness lies in its concise, familiar and easy-to-read format. It answers their question 'Why would my viewers, readers, listeners be interested in this?' before they ask it.

Title

You want to find a hook to catch the editor's or journalist's eye. You then build your press release around that. Make your heading both informative and eye-catching – it could be the only thing that they read.

Format

The Five Ws and One H approach. The five Ws are: who, what, where, when, why, and the H is for how.

Who is your organisation?
What exactly is your story about?
Where is this taking place?
When is it taking place?
Why is this different?
How does it work?

If you don't answer these questions, your press release will probably end up in the bin.

Inverted pyramid

Your approach should be to write the press release with the most important information in the first paragraph. This is the five Ws and the H. Remember that the editor will probably not be able to include all your information and will start cutting paragraphs from the bottom. So, if all your basic information is in the first paragraph and you only get that printed then you've still got your message across!

In the second paragraph you include an exciting quote that elaborates on the basic information in the first paragraph. This allows you to bring life or add a star quality to your release.

The third paragraph can contain a further quote from a different source. You can also give additional information about what you are announcing or some relevant background information on your organisation. Don't distract the reader – keep to the specific focus of this press release.

In the final paragraph you can give details of how to get your leaflet, join your course or book into your event. Do this in one or two sentences.

Include basic information

This means:

☐ Name and address of organisation – usually on press release paper. Have this pre-printed in bulk or make your own by adapting existing headed paper.
☐ Include a name and phone number where editors or journalists can get

more information. As newspaper people work late in the day make sure you include an after-work or a mobile phone number.
- ☐ Indicate the release date. Is it for immediate release or is it embargoed until a specific date?
- ☐ Give the date and place for the story.

The look

You press release must be typed. Indent the paragraphs and use double spacing and wide margins. This gives the editor room to make notes. Keep the left margin straight but leave the right-hand margin unjustified. Keep it to one page, if at all possible. If not, write 'more' at the bottom of page 1 and 'continued' at the top of page 2. Before you send it, check it. Remember it must survive that first 20-second scan or be consigned to the bin.

Press pack

This may sound a rather daunting thing to produce, but with a little preparation it need not be. Your press pack is nothing more elaborate than the materials you send to a journalist when they ask for it. The contents should reinforce your claim to have a story worth publicising. Present the contents in an A4 folder or large white envelope. In Table 15.4 you will find a comprehensive list of items you might include. You will rarely need to include all of these – this list is just to get you thinking.

Table 15.4 Checklist for press pack

- ☐ Press release.
- ☐ Text of statements to be made at conference.
- ☐ One-page fact sheet.
- ☐ One-page summary if a report is being launched.
- ☐ Sheet with quotes from authoritative figures or media reviews.
- ☐ Other marketing materials like booklets or brochures.
- ☐ Sample of product or photo.
- ☐ Specially prepared set of questions and answers on the topic being publicised.
- ☐ Photographs properly captioned on the back.
- ☐ Examples of any promotional materials, e.g., posters, postcards, bumper sticker.
- ☐ Talking points, when aiming at radio or TV programmes you can include a list of interesting questions.

Using your basic tools

Now that you know how to compile your press contact list and how to prepare your press release and press pack, let us concentrate on making the most of them.

Hints to ensure your press release survives

The tone is important

Keep it objective, and avoid too much hype. You may believe your news is a unique and wonderful addition to the world, but you're aiming at one of the most sceptical audiences of all – journalists.

Eliminate typos and mistakes

Proof-read your release and do a spell check. An editor will not be impressed if your release is full of errors. If you are a beginner, ask a colleague to look at it before you send it.

Tailor your press release to different audiences

The editor of a local paper will want the local angle and quotes from local people. The editor of a specialist sports or business magazine will want a focused angle.

Get it to the right person

Put work into your press contact list – make it accurate and right up to date.

The best times to issue a press release

Has your organisation done something new?

Your organisation has just started. You have launched a new campaign. You have just finished a record-breaking year in donations, or you have more donations this year than any previous year. You are offering a new service or operating in a new area. You have a new product or aid which will help people with an illness.

Table 15.5 Common writing mistakes

Use this checklist to examine your writing before signing off on it.

Too many words, verbosity

Check to see if you could get the message across with fewer words. It is tempting to try to impress the reader with complex phrases and lots of words. Resist!

Example: 'It goes without saying, that our staff answer every query.' If you don't need to say it – don't.

Unnecessary superlatives

Remove the 'newest', 'best' and 'greatest' from your work. Instead prove your service or product is the best.

Example: 'Our organisation is famous across the country for the newest ideas in patient care.' Better: 'Our organisation now has six awards for innovations in patient care, more than any other similar organisation.'

Jargon

People who work in the same sector often lapse into jargon because they are all familiar and comfortable with it. It is incomprehensible to outsiders – who are often your target audience.

Example: 'NGOs criticise government for its failure to increase ODA to DAC levels.' Better: 'Voluntary organisations in the non-government sector want the government to increase funding'.

Negative language

By using negative words to make your point you force your reader to go through somersaults to see your meaning.

Example: 'Don't think that the largest donors won't be demanding.' Better: 'Large donors are demanding.'

Vague phrases

Try to use words and phrases which convey a specific meaning. It is very easy to write general, sweeping sentences, which convey little specific information to the reader.

Example: 'Cliff High Trust is an excellent help to parents of ill children.' Why is it excellent? What help can it give? What kinds of illnesses? Better: 'Parents of seriously ill or dying children will get practical support, counselling and advice from a skilled and highly trained staff at Cliff High Trust.'

What is different about your organisation?

Are you a refugee settlement organisation staffed by people who will speak the local language of the refugees? If so, you could be unique and newsworthy.

Do you have a fundraising event or campaign you want to launch?

If the fundraiser is already planning a film première or gala event you should concentrate on maximising publicity for it. It is hard to think up entirely new events in order to attract media attention. Be sure to capitalise on events which are already planned. Contact social magazines and get photos of celebrities attending your event. It is an investment in the future. If your organisation becomes well known for running well-organised and prestigious events, people will take note. You are investing in the future and selling the next event.

Can you take advantage of some current news?

Third world charities operating in a number of countries often take advantage of media interest in a country to highlight their operations there.

Have you done some research to merit press coverage?

If you work in an organisation which funds research, you should produce the results in an easily understood format and get publicity.

Is there a special day or anniversary you could link into?

There are many international or European days which you can exploit to your advantage, e.g. International Volunteers Day, International Women's Day. Call the EU office, or check in a diary.

How to make the most of the phone in getting your publicity

When should I call?

When approaching journalists by phone be aware that you could be interrupting them. They are probably working to a deadline, so find out when deadlines are and take care to avoid them.

Whom should I speak to?

Prepare for your call by calling up the main number in advance and asking with whom you should speak about a particular type of story. They'll give you the name of the relevant journalist and their extension number.

Remember, if you're calling a radio or TV station ask for the producer of the show not the presenter.

How can I make myself clear?

Practise your 'presentation' until you can say it clearly and are comfortable with it. Then inject some enthusiasm. Your aim is to sound more convincing and interesting than 99 per cent of callers.

What do I do if the person isn't interested?

This is a real possibility. Try to get beyond this by anticipating objections or negative responses. The best thing is to prepare a comeback that will give you a second chance. Remember that the person who asks the questions controls the conversation. So listen attentively to what the person says and try to engage them by asking pertinent questions.

Should I call cold or send material out in advance?

People are inclined to pay more attention if they have heard of you, or the name of your organisation rings a bell with them. You can achieve this if they have read something received from you the day before or on morning of your call.

Always remember that people are only half-listening on the phone and are usually trying to get rid of you. So it is always useful to start with 'Did you get my press release?' They will usually look for it then or ask you to send another one.

Should I develop a particular style?

No one style is better than another, but clarity and speaking slowly do improve your chances of the journalist staying on the line. Pace yourself. Don't rush in the first couple of sentences or they will come across as a jumble of words.

How long should I talk?

Generally speaking, your opening line should be around 15–18 seconds. Say enough to interest the other person and then wait. Don't fall into the trap of filling the silence.

Events

Organising an event

No matter what type of event you organise, from a press conference to an exhibition or a major gala evening there is a core list of things which must be done. The secret to successful event management is preparation, attention to detail and double checking everything. You'll add other items to customise this list to different types of events, but this is your starting point. Think of this as your fail-safe list.

Different types of events

1. Press conferences

Inviting the press to a press launch appears to be simple – you just issue the invitations and they come, right? Wrong! Most journalists and editors receive more invitations than they could ever hope to attend. Before you decide to call a press conference it is important to ask yourself a number of questions:

- [ ] Have we got something newsworthy to announce?
- [ ] Have we got someone capable of handling the press questions?
- [ ] Will the press consider it worthwhile coming, or would they be happier with a press release?

Ask yourself this: would the press like the opportunity to question someone to get immediate answers, or will they get access to someone who normally won't meet them.

Location

Choose your location well and think about somewhere that is convenient. It must have parking facilities. Make sure that the room is large enough, well aired and comfortable. Have refreshments available.

Press invitation and press release

Send out your press invitations in good time. Follow up by phone to check if people are coming. Save your press release until the day and give it out at the conference.

If you want to attract their attention, you can send something unusual.

Speakers

Choose your speakers well and instruct them to be brief. For your main speaker, choose someone who knows the issue well and who can explain it convincingly. You could also invite a board member or a celebrity who

Table 15.6 Checklist for organising an event

Venue	access for disabled
	booking form sent in
	insurance
	caterers
	cleaning
	check toilets, cloakrooms
	signage
Personnel	band
	Master of Ceremonies
	artists
	speakers – council or committee
	doorman
	volunteer rota – organise staff list
Photographer	list of different people to be photographed
Room arrangements	tables
	seating
	cutlery
	crockery
Decorations	table centres, napkins, tablecloths
	themed event
Electrics	audiovisual equipment
	TV cameras
	video cameras
	amplification
Food	menu chosen
	costed

	ordered
	tasted
	special requirements, e.g. vegetarian
Drink	costed
	ordered
	tasted
	headwaiter instructed on wine to be opened & when
	corkage charge
Printing	special letterheads
	invitations
	menus
	programme
Guest List	final
Replies in	all in
Provisional numbers for caterers Day before the event – final numbers	
VIPs	number
	special arrangements
Traffic implications	inform police
Facilities for press	
Registration	stand
	personnel
	cash box
	name badges

Media list	for registration
Press advisory, or	
press release	

supports your cause and who will add a media sparkle. Choose a good chairperson or facilitator to run the event and direct questions.

Prepare a running order and make sure everyone has it. Check to see if your press conference is clashing with anything else. Ask one of your journalist contacts to check the news diary.

Setting the time

Many PR people say mid-morning is best as it allows you to catch the evening papers and possibly the early evening radio or TV news.

The day

Arrive early on the day and check all the physical arrangements are in place. Arrange the chairs to suit the number you are expecting. Don't have 100 chairs in the room if you are only expecting about ten people: it can make a good event look badly attended.

Clearly display your organisation's name at the check-in and behind the speakers. Use banners, posters or photographs. Place someone near the door to meet and greet people and to get their names. This person can distribute the press pack. If a journalist fails to turn up, mail the press pack and follow up with a phone call.

Photo opportunity

A photo opportunity focuses, not surprisingly, on providing a good picture. Your event can be solely a photo opportunity or a subsection of a press conference or press launch.

When sending out the notice to the press, use your press release, but with two important differences: emphasise the visual impact and send it directly to the *photo desk* or *photo editor* of the newspaper:

When setting up the photo opportunity think like a photographer, not like a journalist. To help you do this collect photographs from national and local papers. Concentrate on the ones which struck you first. In addition to the general pages of the newspaper, collect photos from the society pages, business pages and from magazines. They will make a handy reference for you and, when stuck for ideas, you can use them to stimulate your creative ideas.

It is a good idea to collect photos associated with organisations similar to your own. That way you have a very good idea of what has already been presented to the photo editors and can avoid duplication.

How to set up a good photo

Remember that press photographers will always look for their own angle and object to being spoon-fed. On the other hand, they do expect you to lay something on. The challenge is to find a happy medium whereby you provide a number of opportunities, but let them decide on the final shot.

While you must be creative, don't go over the top. Photographers are attracted by celebrities, so if you have any associated with your organisation get them to come along.

Use props to make it more unusual. Get large cut-out numbers if you are celebrating an anniversary or announcing a fundraising drive to raise a targeted amount. Photographers love animals and children, but remember they can be unpredictable and uncontrollable.

Always have your own photographer. While the national papers will always use their own photographer's work, local papers may use your shots! And you will have professional photographs for your newsletter and for your file for future sponsorship proposals or fundraising pitches.

Remember to talk to the photographers. Ask them if there is anything in particular they want. Try to accommodate them. Make sure they have the names of the people they are photographing. A one-page brief can be very helpful to them.

Exhibitions

Many not for profits take stands at major conferences or exhibitions. They do so to increase their profile among a select target group. They often use it as a way of recruiting volunteer or raising awareness of a particular campaign or issue.

Careful thought is needed before booking a stand. It is important to be clear about why you are taking it. Don't get involved simply because everyone else is. It should be a part of your overall PR strategy for the year. Booking a stand is not a decision to be taken without considering the implications of resourcing it. You'll need staff or volunteers to attend, materials to give out and publicity materials to decorate the stand.

The nineteen steps in Table 15.7 will take you through all the angles. Read them before making a final decision.

Publications

Find out what your readers want

Ask readers to let you know what they like and dislike. Include reply coupons on brochures or annual reports. Monitor how your publications are used. Actively carry out reader research.

Target your publications

You will need to produce different publications for donors. Donors want their support to be given credit. They want up-to-date information about what the organisation is doing and what has been done with their money. They like good news and want to know that their contribution is helping people. Although some charities like to use negative images for their shock value, generally, donors don't like this approach.

Campaign PR and organising a protest

Sometimes in the not for profit sector one has to organise a protest to draw attention to an issue. Before deciding on a protest you should consider a number of questions:

- ☐ Are my other PR strategies working?
- ☐ Is our organisation or cause getting enough public attention? If not, do we need to get a short, sharp focus?
- ☐ Are we up against a deadline?
- ☐ Is someone or some organisation doing something which will adversely affect our supporters, members and we have no time left? If we don't do something dramatic quickly, we're lost.
- ☐ Is our group or band of supporters exhausted and is support dwindling away? If you feel something motivating, large and emotive is called for, organise a public protest.

Type of protest

It is important to state clearly that only non-violent protests should be carried out.

Demonstrations and marches

Quite simply, you are trying to get a large number of people out onto the street to highlight your issue or campaign. People can gather in one place at a rally or protest on the move in a march. You should try to structure it with a start and an end time, a slot for speakers or a symbolic gesture, like

Table 15.7 Nineteen steps to successful exhibitions

---

1. Decision to Exhibit
Be clear why you are spending money (on an exhibition stand, props, personnel, travel and accommodation) before you sign up. The cost of the stand is not the only cost, it is just the beginning.

2. Be Clear about Your Target Group
Make this clear to everyone involved in the decision and in resourcing the stand. Be clear whether you are developing a market or merely on a fishing expedition.

3. Reserve Your Location
Familiarise yourself with the exhibition centre and see a map of the entire layout of stands. Make sure your stand is in an appropriate section. If you're an educational charity you don't want to end up with the financial services group.

Choose a size of stand in keeping with your overall budget.

4. Decide Your Budget
Remember to consider everything, including stand rental or construction, promotional materials, costs of personnel and any advertising or public relations costs.

5. Agree Design
Don't take shortcuts with the design of the stand. Use the overall stand construction company or if necessary get your own. Don't be cheap. It is your image on show here. If the cost is too hard for the financial people in your organisation to swallow – don't get involved in the exhibition at all.

6. Decide on Products to be Displayed
Select a range of products well in advance. Don't leave it to the last minute otherwise your stand may look like a bring and buy sale.

7. Prepare Special Items
You may decide to highlight a special product or service. Order this well in advance and try it out. Make sure the personnel on the stand are totally familiar with it.

8. Organise Transport
If you have lots of literature or any bulky items, book transport for the journey to and from the exhibition.

9. Order Special Items
You may want flowers, extra chairs, power points, water machine, cleaning materials.

10. Insurance
Check the organiser's insurance. Do you need coverage of your own?

11. Your Name Board
Do you have to supply your own or give your name to the organiser?

12. Select Personnel

Exercise great care in who you put on an exhibition stand. They are your organisation's ambassadors. They must look good, speak well, know the organisation and be good, clear communicators. Don't choose shy people, it is an excruciating experience for them! Arrange a roster so that people get breaks during the day and the stand remains covered at all times.

13. Brief Personnel

Make sure everyone knows why they are there. Brief them on the objectives for your participation in the exhibition. Tell them who the target groups are. Ensure they are totally familiar with your products and services on display.

14. Training

Have a day's training for the personnel on the stand, both staff and volunteers. Treat them like a team and they'll perform as one.

15. Prepare Guest List

This is your chance to shine. Make sure all the right people see the organisation at its best. Invite council members, staff, key volunteers, relevant supporters or donors. Inform your media contacts.

16. Mention in Programme or Catalogue

The programme will last long after the exhibition is over and so it is vital that you are listed – complete with your address and phone number. You may want to consider taking an advert if there is some special product or service you want to promote. Always ask for a charity rate.

17. Get a Photograph of Your Stand

After all this work make sure you record the event. You'll be able to use photographs in your newsletter or in a sponsorship proposal at a later time.

18. Make a Record of Visitors to Your Stand

Collect names and addresses of all visitors and enquiries. They will be useful for direct mail, selling your newsletter, inviting to further events.

Print up special enquiry forms. Discuss data needed with your direct mail colleagues.

19. Thank Your Stand Personnel

Have a token or present ready to give them at the end of the day. They've worked hard and they'll really appreciate it. Get your team together afterwards and listen to their views. They will be your best teacher. Revisit your original plan, objectives and target groups. Did you meet your objectives and did you reach your target groups? The answers to these questions will help you to decide about taking a stand at another exhibition.

lighting candles. For large events your success may be judged by the numbers who turn up, as this gives an indication of public support. So be careful. If only a small number turn up and you billed it as an event anticipating thousands, you'll look like a failure. And this will demoralise your campaign supporters.

Table 15.8 Some practical points for campaign public relations

☐ Plan – plan – plan.

☐ Have a leader or co-ordinator.

☐ Delegate tasks to individuals and make them responsible for their completion.

☐ Inform the police.

☐ Make banners, placards.

☐ Make and distribute cheap flyers.

☐ Inform the media, use your media list.

☐ Prepare press releases clearly stating your aims.

☐ Put someone in charge of getting people to turn up. Get them to gather a group around them who will work the phones.

☐ Invite politicians, local, national and MEPs.

☐ Hire a photographer.

Quick ways to get publicity

Write a letter to the editor

Always read the letters to the editor columns in the major nationals and any specialist magazines relevant to your sector, e.g., the medical magazines if you are a health charity. This way you are on top of any breaking story. You can use the letters page to highlight an issue of concern to your organisation. It can be useful to initiate and sustain an ongoing debate through letters. Phone your council members or supporters and motivate them to write. It is useful to discover who are the good creative letter writers in your organisation. Encourage them. Ask them to be brief, original and to the point. Offer to type their letter, if they can't.

Phone-ins

Ask one of your supporters to phone a local radio station to talk about an event or campaign you want to publicise. Local radio stations respond more readily to a local angle.

Notice board or radio and TV

Phone your local stations and find out if they have a community notice board. If they do, how much notice is required and what day is it broadcast?

Advertisements

If you want to be certain of coverage, then pay for it. Sometimes if coverage is crucial to the success of an event, the best action is to place newspaper, radio or TV ads. You can ask for a charity discount or try to get your ad sponsored.

Summary points

1. Public relations must work hand in glove with fundraising as a vital support.
2. You must plan your public relations strategy.
3. There are three basic public relations tools – press contact list, press release and press pack.
4. Build up your press contact list.
5. Remember your five W's and one H approach to your press releases.
6. Use your checklist for your press pack.
7. Know the best times to issue press materials.
8. Use your checklist for all your public relations events.
9. Take care to follow the steps outlined to organise a successful press conference or photo opportunity.
10. Use the all-embracing 20 steps to ensure exhibition success.
11. Remember the practical points before launching your protest campaign.

16

WRITE YOUR OWN FUNDRAISING AND PUBLIC RELATIONS PLANS

Introduction

You are now ready to write your own plans. This chapter will guide you through each stage. Please refer to earlier chapter for details.

Mission statement

First you must define your mission statement for *your* work. One definition I came across recently which I've adapted for a fundraiser is as follows:

> '*A vivid picture of an ambitious, desirable future state that is connected to the donor and better in some way than the current state.*'

Table 16.1 Quick guide to your plan

☐ Write your mission statement.

☐ Survey and categorise sources of income and get an historical perspective by examining income over last five years.

☐ Step back and identify the strengths, weaknesses, opportunities and threats (SWOT analysis).

☐ Take each fundraising activity and decide which are the 'stars' and which the 'dead dogs' (portfolio analysis).

☐ Use the SMART approach to set your goals.

☐ Allocate time in the next twelve months to achieve your goals.

Table 16.2 My job

Mission statement

That's inspiring – isn't it? Now write your own.

Remember, your ideal mission statement should be clear, memorable, aligned with your organisation's overall values, linked to donors' needs and, above all, challenging.

Survey sources of income

Having stated your mission you now need to look at your present situation and assess it.

First, survey your existing sources of income and fill in Table 16.3. This will help you categorise your different fundraising activities – this is a useful precursor to doing the portfolio analysis later. To get a more complete picture you can go on to fill in a survey of income over the past five years. Do this using Table 16.4. This is particularly useful for a new fundraiser or a new member of a fundraising committee.

Take a step back: SWOT analysis

If you want to take a step back and have a look at your work overall you'll find the SWOT analysis very useful. You can do it on your own, but for best results involve your co-workers or the members of your fundraising or PR committee. Use Figures 16.1 and 16.2.

Rate your projects: portfolio analysis

It is useful to take each fundraising or PR project separately and decide where it fits in a portfolio analysis.

Table 16.3 Survey of existing income

Source of Income Change Last Year	£ Amount	% Total Income	£ Amount Last Year
Voluntary Income			
Direct Mail Campaigns			
1.			
2.			
3.			
4.			
Major Gifts			
Workplace Giving			
Covenants			
Bequests			
Special Events			
☐ Large-scale			
1.			
2.			
3.			
4.			
☐ Small-scale Total			
Grants			
Government			
1.			
2.			

3.

4.

Foundations/Trusts

1.

2.

3.

4.

Corporate Donations

1.

2.

3.

4.

Sponsorship

1.

2.

3.

TOTALS

Decide which of your projects are your stars and your dead dogs. It is important to know this so that you can concentrate on your stars. This exercise can throw new light on some worrying problems which have been frustrating you. If they emerge as dead dogs you can then proceed to discontinue them. Use Figures 16.3 and 16.4.

Getting things done: setting goals

Now you know where your existing funds come from, the relative strengths and weaknesses of all your fundraising activities and you have decided what you want to achieve in the next twelve months.

Table 16.4 Total income over last four years

Source of Income	Year 1 (%)	Year 2 (%)	Year 3 (%)	Year 4 (%)
Voluntary Income				
Direct Mail Campaigns				
1.				
2.				
3.				
4.				
Major Gifts				
Workplace Giving				
Covenants				
Bequests				
Special Events				
☐ Large-scale				
1.				
2.				
3.				
4.				
☐ Small-scale Total				
Grants				
Government				
1.				
2.				
3.				

4.	
Foundations/ Trusts	
1.	
2.	
3.	
4.	
Corporate Donations	
1.	
2.	
3.	
4.	
Sponsorship	
1.	
2.	
3.	
TOTALS	

You are ready to set your goals. Fill in the chart and set SMART goals. Use Tables 16.5 and 16.6.

Make time

All the goals in the world will amount to nothing if you don't allocate specific times to do them. Set deadlines for each stage of your projects using Tables 16.7 and 16.8.

Internal Strengths	External Opportunities
1	1
2	2
3	3
4	4
5	5
6	6
7	7
8	8
9	9
10	10
Internal Weaknesses	**External Threat**
1	1
2	2
3	3
4	4
5	5
6	6
7	7
8	8
9	9
10	10

Figure 16.1 SWOT analysis: fundraising

Internal Strengths	External Opportunities
1	1
2	2
3	3
4	4
5	5
6	6
7	7
8	8
9	9
10	10
Internal Weaknesses	External Threat
1	1
2	2
3	3
4	4
5	5
6	6
7	7
8	8
9	9
10	10

Figure 16.2 SWOT analysis: public relations

FUNDRAISING YIELD HIGH	FUNDRAISING YIELD LOW

H   **STARS**
I   1
G   2
H   3
      4
      5
E
F
F
O
R
T
	PROBLEM CHILDREN
	1
	2
	3
	4
	5

L   **CASH COWS**
O   1
W   2
      3
      4
      5
E
F
F
O
R
T
	DEAD DOGS
	1
	2
	3
	4
	5

Figure 16.3 Portfolio analysis: fundraising

FUNDRAISING YIELD	FUNDRAISING YIELD
HIGH	**LOW**
H **STARS**	**PROBLEM CHILDREN**
I 1	1
G 2	2
H 3	3
4	4
5	5
E	
F	
F	
O	
R	
T	
L **CASH COWS**	**DEAD DOGS**
O 1	1
W 2	2
3	3
4	4
5	5
E	
F	
F	
O	
R	
T	

Figure 16.4 Portfolio analysis: public relations

Table 16.5 Setting fundraising goals the SMART way

Specific Goals	Quantify Goal	Is It Achievable?	Result Expected	Time Deadline
1 GOAL				
2 GOAL				
3 GOAL				
4 GOAL				
5 GOAL				
6 GOAL				

7 GOAL				
8 GOAL				
9 GOAL				
10 GOAL				

Table 16.6 Setting public relations goals the SMART way

Specific Goals	Quantify Goal	Is It Achievable?	Result Expected	Time Deadline
1 GOAL				
2 GOAL				
3 GOAL				
4 GOAL				
5 GOAL				
6 GOAL				

7 GOAL				
8 GOAL				
9 GOAL				
10 GOAL				

Table 16.7 Allocate time to achieve your annual fundraising goals

Goals	Jan/ Feb	Mar/ Apr	May/ Jun	Jul/ Aug	Sept/ Oct	Nov/ Dec
1						
2						
3						
4						
5						
6						

7						
8						
9						
10						

Table 16.8 Allocate time to achieve your annual public relations goals

Goals	Jan/ Feb	Mar/ Apr	May/ Jun	Jul/ Aug	Sept/ Oct	Nov/ Dec
1						
2						
3						
4						
5						
6						

7						
8						
9						
10						

A GUIDE TO FUNDRAISING AND PUBLIC RELATIONS RESOURCES

Reading materials

Bird, Drayton, *Commonsense Direct Marketing*, Kogan Page.

Bruce, Ian, *Meeting Need: Successful Charity Marketing*, ICSA Publishing.

Burnett, Ken, *Relationship Fundraising*, The White Lion Press Ltd.

Charities Administration, *A Manual for Charities and Voluntary Organisations*, ICSA Publishing.

Courtney, Roger, *Managing Voluntary Organisations: New Approaches*, ICSA Publishing

Covey, Stephen R., *The Seven Habits of Highly Effective People*, Fireside – Simon & Schuster.

Drucker, Peter F., *Managing the Nonprofit Organisation*, HarperCollins Publishers.

Gordon Lewis, Herschell, *How to Write Powerful Fundraising Letters*, Pluribus Press.

Harrison, John, *Managing Charitable Investments*, ICSA Publishing.

Jefkins, Frank, *The Secrets of Successful Direct Response Marketing*, Heinemann Professional Publishing.

Laurie, Alan, *The Complete Guide to Business and Strategic Planning for Voluntary Organisations*, Directory of Social Change Publication.

Manley, Keith, *Financial Management for Charities & Voluntary Organisations*, ICSA Publishing.

Mullin, Redmond, *Foundations for Fundraising*, ICSA Publishing.

Palmer, Paul and Jenny Harrow, *Rethinking Charity Trusteeship: Beyond the Trustee's Handbook*, ICSA Publishing.

Peters, Thomas J. and Robert H. Waterman Jr, *In Search of Excellence*, Harper & Row Publishers.

Pharoah, Cathy, ed., *Dimensions of The Voluntary Sector* – 1997 Edition. Charities Aid Foundation, Kings Hill, West Malling, Kent ME19 4TA.

Seymour, Harold J., *Designs for Fundraising*, Fundraising Institute.

Sprinkel Grace, Kay, *Beyond Fundraising*, Wiley Publishers.

Warwick, Mal, *Raising Money by Mail*, Strathmoor Press.

Williams, Stephen, *Charities and Taxation*, ICSA Publishing.

Wise, David, *Performance Measurement for Charities*, ICSA Publishing.

Wolf, Thomas, *Managing a Nonprofit Organisation*, Prentice Hall.

Magazines

Advancing Philanthropy is published quarterly by the National Society of Fundraising Executives, 1101 King Street, Suite 700, Alexandria, VA 22314 USA.

Charity Magazine is produced under licence from the Charities Aid Foundation. It is published by Voluntary Sector Services Centurion Press Ltd. in association with Indigo Publishing Ltd. Charity, BMS, Merlin Way, North Weald Industrial Estate, Epping, Essex CM16 6HR. Tel: 01992 523943.

Fundraising Management Magazine is published monthly by HOKE Communications Inc, at 224 Seventh Street, Garden City, New York 11530–5771.

IPR and Journal of the IPR; IPR Update: The Newsletter of The Institute of Public Relations. The Old Trading House, 15 Nortburgh Street, London EC1V 0PR. Tel: 0171 253 5151.

NCVO News Subscriptions at Regents' Wharf, 8 All Saints Street, London N1 9RL.

NCVO News, magazine of the National Council for Voluntary Organisations. Tel: 0171 713 6161.

Third Sector is published by Arts Publishing International Ltd. Third Sector Subscriptions Department, Arts Publishing International Ltd. Freepost LON 6577, London E1 7BR. Tel: 0171 237 0066.

Useful addresses

Direct mail

Direct Marketing Association (UK) Ltd
Haymarket House, 1 Oxendon Street, London SW1Y 4EE
Tel: 0171 321 2525.
The Direct Marketing Association (UK) Ltd is the single trade body representing all those involved in direct marketing in the UK. Its mission is to 'represent the best interests of members by raising the statue of the Direct Marketing Industry and giving the consumer trust and confidence in Direct Marketing'. The DMA can give you lists of direct marketing agencies from its Membership Directory. It also has training events and a full library service.

Royal Mail
The Royal Mail provides an excellent range of information leaflets. Their 'Direct Marketing Services Guide' is a particularly useful folder with four leaflets covering campaign planning, targeting and databases and listing of royal mail services. To get information on any Royal Mail Services, call their local sales centre on 0345 950 950.

The Advertising Association
Abford House, 15 Wilton Road, London SW1V 1NJ
Tel: 0171 828 2771. Fax: 0171 931 0376.
The Advertising Association is a federation of 27 trade associations and professional bodies representing advertisers, agencies, the media and support services. It is the only body which speaks for all sides of an industry worth £10 billion.

Association of Household Distributors
36 Frogmore Street, Tring, Hertfordshire HP23 5AU
Tel: 01442 890991. Fax: 01442 890992
The trade association for door-to-door distribution. Members agree to abide by the Code of Practice and Guidelines. An annual free publication 'The Letterbox Marketing Handbook', is available and provides background details on all members and details of all numbers.

The Association of Media & Communications Specialists
163 Rickmansworth High Street, Rickmansworth WD3 1AY
Tel: 01923 720628. Fax: 01923 711982.
The Association of Media & Communications Specialists aims to encourage the development of media opportunities, as well as ensuring the need for greater accountability and measurement in assessing communication value. The association also ensures professional standards and the furtherance of knowledge on the commercial communication process amongst its members and their staff.

The Direct Mail Accreditation and Recognition Centre
248 Tottenham Court Road, London W1P 9AD
Tel: 0171 631 0904. Fax: 0171 631 0859.
The DMARC is an independent body that confers 'recognised status' on suppliers of direct mail services who meet the highest of ethical and professional standards, and as such is the sign to look for. A list of suppliers is available from them.

The Direct Mail Information Service
5 Carlisle Street, London W1V 6JX
Tel: 0171 494 0483. Fax: 0171 494 0455.
The Direct Mail Information Service is the source of industry statistics, research and general information.

The Institute of Direct Marketing
1 Park Road, Teddington, Middlesex TW11 0AR
Tel: 0181 977 5705. Fax: 0181 943 2535.
Responsible for organising the IDM Direct Marketing Diploma, the institute also organises other educational initiatives to improve the knowledge of direct marketing.

The Mailing Preference Service
5 Reef House, Plantation Wharf, London SW11 3UF
Tel: 0171 738 1625. Fax: 0171 978 4918.
The MPS allows consumers to decrease or increase the amount of direct mail they receive. Registration is free to the public. As a subscriber to this service, businesses can use these lists of consumers to clean their mailing lists, making them more effective.

The Office of the Data Protection Registrar
Wycliffe House, Water Lane, Wilmslow, Cheshire SK9 5AF
Tel: 01625 535711. Fax: 01625 524510.
The Office of the Data Protection Registrar is the government body that provides guidance on the laws governing the holding and use of personal data, including that which is used for direct mail purposes.

Grants

The National Lottery
Millennium Commission. Tel: 0171 880 2201.
National Lottery Arts Council. Tel: 0171 333 0100.
National Lottery Heritage Board. Tel: 0171 930 0963. Fax: 0171 930 0968.
Application enquiries. Tel: 0171 747 2082/3/4/5/6/7.
National Lottery Sports Board. Tel: 0171 388 1277. Fax: 0171 387 1999 (advice on applications 2–5 pm).

NLCB England. Tel: 0116 258–7000. Fax: 0116 255–7398/9.
NLCB Northern Ireland. Tel: 0 1232 551455. Fax: 0 1232 551444.
NLCB Scotland. Tel: 0131 221 7100. Fax: 0131 221 7120.
NLCB Wales. Tel: 01686 621644. Fax: 01686 621534.

Regional Offices
East Midlands. Tel: 0115 959 8866.
Eastern. Tel: 01223 506016.
Greater London. Tel: 0171 747 5205.
North East. Tel: 0191 514 2823.
North West. Tel: 01925 242530.
South East. Tel: 0171 747 5204.
South West. Tel: 01392 491139.
West Midland. Tel: 0121 693 4757.
Yorkshire & Humberside. Tel: 0113 244 0358.

Association of Charitable Foundations
4 Bloomsbury Square, London WC1A 2RL
Tel: 0171 404 1338

Association of Community Trusts & Foundations (Actaf)
4 Bloomsbury Square, London WC1A 2RL
Tel: 0171 404 1338.

Joseph Rowntree Foundation
The Homestead, 40 Water End, York, YO3 6LP
Tel: 01904 654328
Publications list available.

Training

Organisations offering training in fundraising:

Directory of Social Change
24 Stephenson Way, London NW1 2DP
Book orders. Tel: 0171 209 5151.

Institute of Charity Fundraising Managers
208 Market Towers, Nine Elms Lane, London SW8 5NQ
Tel: 0171 627 3436

London Voluntary Service Council
356 Holloway Road, London N7 6PA
Tel: 0171 7008107
Funding advice and training for London-based organisations.

Management Centre
9–15 Blackett Street, Newcastle upon Tyne NE1 5BS.
Management consultancy and training organisation working for non-profit bodies.

Local councils for voluntary service or rural community councils often run fundraising courses.

National Council For Voluntary Organisations (NCVO)
NCVO, Regent's Wharf, 8 All Saints Street, London N1 9RL
Tel: 0171 713 6161. Fax: 0171 713 6300
NCVO has an active network of over 700 voluntary organisations. It represents the views of the voluntary sector to government, the EC and the Charity Commission. It provides high-quality research and analysis of the sector. It offers a range of constantly expanding advice and consultancy services to help voluntary organisations from start-up to long-term development. It promotes quality standards in training and development for the voluntary sector. It brings together information on key developments in the sector through a range of conferences, seminars and publications.

The National Centre for Volunteering
Carriage Row, 183 Eversholt Street, London NW1 1BU
Tel: 0171 388 9888

Northern Ireland Council of Voluntary Action
127 Ormeau Road, Belfast BT7 1SH
Tel: 01232 321224

Scottish Council for Voluntary Organisations
18–19 Claremont Crescent, Edinburgh EH7 4QD
Tel: 0131 556 3882.

Wales Council for Voluntary Action
Llys Ifor, Crescent Road, Caerphilly, Mid Glamorgan CF8 1XL
Tel: 01222 869224.

Charities Advisory Trust
Radius Works, Back Lane, London NW3 1HL
Tel: 0171–794–9835.
Advises on all aspects of charity trading.

Charity Commission Offices
St Albans House, 57–60 Haymarket, London SW1Y 4QX
Tel: 0171 210 4477
Graeme House, Derby Square, Liverpool L2 7SB

Tel: 0151 227 3191
Woodfield House, Tangier, Taunton, Somerset TA1 4BL
Tel: 01823 345000.
Helpline: 0171 210 4630 assists charities requiring information or guidelines on the new regulations concerning fundraising.

Charities Aid Foundation (CAF)
CAF, Kings Hill, West Malling, Kent ME19 4TA
Tel: 01732 520 000 Fax: 01732 520 001
http://www.charitynet.org
e-mail: enquiries@caf.charitynet.org
CAF is a registered charity which provides services that are both charitable and financial. They work to help donors make the most of their giving and charities make the most of their resources in the UK and overseas. They do this by bringing together resources, skills and knowledge from both the charitable and financial sectors.

Public Relations

Reuter Foundation
85 Fleet Street, London EC4P 4AJ
Tel: 0171 542 7962
Offers media relations workshops designed to help charities make better use of the news media. The workshop is conducted by professionals, is free of charge and lasts for one day. The emphasis is on practical training with sessions on writing news releases and interview techniques for the broadcast media.

The Media Trust
The Media Trust, 3–6 Alfred Place, London WC1E 7EB
Tel: 0171 637 4747 Fax: 0171 637 5757
e-mail mediatrust@easynet.co.uk
The Media Trust produces broadcast programmes and creates programme opportunities for and about the voluntary sector. It matches the skills and resources of the media and public relations industry to the communication needs of charities and voluntary organisations. It provides information, training and contacts by producing print and on-line information, and by organising seminars and conferences for the voluntary sector and the media.

The Institute of Public Relations
The Old Trading House, 15 Northburgh Street, London EC1V 0PR.
Tel: 0171 253 5151
This is the professional body which represents around 5,000 PR professionals Membership entitles you to publications, access to various services and to a network of others working in the area.

Consultants

Association of Fundraising Consultants
The Grove, Harpenden, Herts AL5 1AH.
Tel: 01582 762446.

Canning and Associates
25 Upper Mount Street, Dublin 2, Ireland
Tel: 353 1 6760084

INDEX